About Access Archaeology

Access Archaeology offers a different publishing model for specialist academic material that might traditionally prove commercially unviable, perhaps due to its sheer extent or volume of colour content, or simply due to its relatively niche field of interest.

All *Access Archaeology* publications are available in open-access e-pdf format and in (on-demand) print format. The open-access model supports dissemination in areas of the world where budgets are more severely limited, and also allows individual academics from all over the world the chance to access the material privately, rather than relying solely on their university or public library. Print copies, nevertheless, remain available to individuals and institutions who need or prefer them.

The material is professionally refereed, but not peer reviewed. Copy-editing takes place prior to submission of the work for publication and is the responsibility of the author. Academics who are able to supply print-ready material are not charged any fee to publish (including making the material available in open-access). In some instances the material is type-set in-house and in these cases a small charge is passed on for layout work.

This model works for us as a publisher because we are able to publish specialist work with relatively little editorial investment. Our core effort goes into promoting the material, both in open-access and print, where *Access Archaeology* books get the same level of attention as our core peer-reviewed imprint by being included in marketing e-alerts, print catalogues, displays at academic conferences and more, supported by professional distribution worldwide.

Open-access allows for greater dissemination of the academic work than traditional print models, even lithographic printing, could ever hope to support. It is common for a new open-access e-pdf to be downloaded several hundred times in its first month since appearing on our website. Print sales of such specialist material would take years to match this figure, if indeed it ever would.

By printing 'on-demand', meanwhile, (or, as is generally the case, maintaining minimum stock quantities as small as two), we are able to ensure orders for print copies can be fulfilled without having to invest in great quantities of stock in advance. The quality of such printing has moved forward radically, even in the last few years, vastly increasing the fidelity of images (highly important in archaeology) and making colour printing more economical.

Access Archaeology is a vehicle that allows us to publish useful research, be it a PhD thesis, a catalogue of archaeological material or data, in a model that does not cost more than the income it generates.

This model may well evolve over time, but its ambition will always remain to publish archaeological material that would prove commercially unviable in traditional publishing models, without passing the expense on to the academic (author or reader).

Shipwrecks and Provenance

in-situ timber sampling protocols

with a focus on wrecks of the Iberian shipbuilding tradition

Sara A. Rich, Nigel Nayling, Garry Momber and Ana Crespo Solana

Access Archaeology

Archaeopress Publishing Ltd
Gordon House
276 Banbury Road
Oxford OX2 7ED

www.archaeopress.com

ISBN 978 1 78491 717 3
ISBN 978 1 78491 718 0 (e-Pdf)

© Archaeopress and the individual authors 2017

Printed and bound in Great Britain by
Marston Book Services Ltd, Oxfordshire

All rights reserved. No part of this book may be reproduced or transmitted,
in any form or by any means, electronic, mechanical, photocopying or otherwise,
without the prior written permission of the copyright owners.

Contents

List of Figures..iii
Acknowledgements v
Chapter 1. The Uniquely Problematic Shipwrecks of the Equally Problematic 'Age of Discovery' 1
1.1. Historical Background..1
1.2. Emergent oceangoing ship types 3
    1.2.1. Galleon 4
    1.2.2. *Nao, nau*, carrack..5
    1.2.3. Caravel 5
1.3. What it means to be 'Iberian' 5
1.4. Treasure and archaeology 6
Chapter 2. Timber Samples and Dendroprovenance... 9
2.1. Scientific analyses..11
    2.1.1. Dendrochronology 12
    2.1.2. Dendroarchaeology 12
    2.1.3. DNA 13
    2.1.4. Geochemistry 13
    2.1.5. Anatomical and structural markers 14
Chapter 3. Sampling and Sub-sampling 15
3.1. Selection 16
    3.1.1. Assemblage and preservation 20
    3.1.2. Sampling underwater 22
    3.1.3. Sampling on land 30
3.2. Post-excavation processing..31
    3.2.1. Cleaning 31
    3.2.2. Visual recording 32
    3.2.3. Text-based description..33
    3.2.4. Storage 34
    3.2.5. Database management 34
3.3. Sub-sampling...36
    3.3.1. Dendrochronology 36
    3.3.2. Dendroarchaeology 36
    3.3.1. DNA 37
    3.3.4. Geochemistry 37

    3.3.5. Anatomical and structural markers 37

    3.3.6. Radiocarbon (^{14}C) 38

Chapter 4. Legal Considerations 39

4.1. Heritage and environmental organizations 39

4.2. Approved Code of Practice (ACoP) for Scientific and Archaeological Diving Projects 40

    4.2.1. Diving Project Plan 40

    4.2.2. Risk Assessments 41

4.3. Receiver of Wreck 41

4.4. Follow-up reports and archiving 42

Chapter 5. Ethical Considerations 43

5.1. UNESCO and *in-situ* preservation 43

5.2. Destruction or displacement? 44

5.3. Dissemination 45

Chapter 6. Conclusions 47

6.1. Future of scientific and maritime archaeologies 47

6.2. Importance of inter- and multi-disciplinary collaboration 48

Glossary 51

Bibliography 57

List of Figures

Figure 1. Map of main North Atlantic ocean currents, corresponding with trade winds and Iberian trans-Atlantic sailing routes from the late 15th century. Map prepared by María José García Rodríguez with data from Ana Crespo Solana, © ForSEAdiscovery Project, 2016 3

Figure 2. Distribution map of known sixteenth to eighteenth-century Iberian shipwrecks in the Atlantic Ocean and the Pacific coast of the Americas. Of these, 698 are known from historical records and 216 from archaeological investigations. The western Pacific and Indian Oceans surely harbor comparable numbers of vessels, although fewer have been identified and investigated as of yet. The Global Shipwrecks Database, from which this map was produced, seeks to continually build upon its existing dataset and incorporate other databases of Iberian shipwreck sites around the world. Map prepared by María José García Rodríguez with data from Ana Crespo Solana, © ForSEAdiscovery Project, 2016 4

Figure 3. Supposed shipwreck timber from a galleon of the 1986 Spanish *armada* that appeared on the online auction site Ebay in 2015 after having washed up on the Scottish coast as flotsam 7

Figure 4. Examples of research questions that could form the basis for interrogating a wooden shipwreck site through a systematic timber sampling campaign 10

Figure 5. Table with descriptions of analytical dendroprovenance methods and what each requires from a wood sample 11

Figure 6. Examples of questions to consider when developing an underwater timber sampling strategy 15

Figure 7. Slivers of transverse sections of pine (*Pinus* sp.; left) and deciduous oak (*Quercus* subg. *quercus*; right), demonstrating the visible differentiating features: color, sharper distinctions between annual growth rings in pine, porous earlywood in oak, and medullary rays in oak. Photograph © Sara Rich, 2017 17

Figure 8. Schematic diagram of the transverse section of deciduous oak. Diagram © Sara Rich, 2017 ... 17

Figure 9. Schematic diagram of the transverse section of a coniferous wood. Diagram © Sara Rich, 2017 ... 18

Figure 10. Schematic diagram of the radial conversion of deciduous oak. Diagram © Sara Rich, 2017 19

Figure 11. Schematic diagram of the tangential conversion of a coniferous wood. Diagram © Sara Rich, 2017 20

Figure 12. Diver photographs ship timbers *in situ* at the Yarmouth Roads shipwreck site (Isle of Wight, UK). These digital photographs contribute to the ongoing 3D model of the site. Photograph by Beñat Eguíluz Miranda, © Maritime Archaeology, Ltd., 2016 21

Figure 13. Samples of framing elements from two different shipwrecks; all four sampled timbers were converted from fast-grown, short-lived oak trees. Left: excavated samples in good condition with preserved sapwood on elongated corners from the bow of the Yarmouth Roads shipwreck (Isle of Wight, UK). Right: exposed teredo-ridden samples with preserved sapwood (lighter in colour) from the wrecked sixteenth-century galleon at Ribadeo (Galicia, Spain). Photographs by Sara Rich, © Maritime Archaeology, Ltd., 2015 23

Figure 14. Diver removes a cross-section of pine hull planking from the wrecked eighteenth-century frigate *La Santa Maria Magdalena* (Galicia, Spain). The ends of the planking were not accessible, so samples were removed from the center. Photograph by Adolfo Miguel Martins, © Maritime Archaeology, Ltd., 2015. 24

Figure 15. Example of the step-by-step procedure for removing a wood sample from a shipwreck underwater...25

Figure 16. A series of sampled hull planks *in situ* at the Yarmouth Roads shipwreck (Isle of Wight, UK) demonstrating tangential conversion, which preserves only a few annual growth rings of relatively slow-grown and moderately long-lived trees. Samples were removed from the ends of the exposed planks. Photograph by Martin Davies, © Martin Davies and Maritime Archaeology, Ltd., 2016 26

Figure 17. Cross-sections removed from different parts of the same timber may show different records of the parent tree's growth. Cross-sections from limbs or further up the stem will be more likely to display warped ring-width patterns due to branching and knots, while those taken from areas corresponding with the base of the stem will be more likely to display a ring-width pattern that corresponds more accurately with the whole tree's growth (left). Those sampling will do well to keep in mind where a certain ship timber would have originated within the parent tree. Ring-width patterns may also demonstrate the original landscape, such as forested or open, and whether or not the parent tree had been managed through coppicing (right). Drawing © Sara Rich, 2017...27

Figure 18. Hull planking samples from two different shipwrecks; each sample was converted from a slow-grown, long-lived tree. Top: tangentially converted pine planking with preserved sapwood (on left) from the wrecked eighteenth-century frigate *La Santa Maria Magdalena* (Galicia, Spain). Bottom: radially converted oak planking with preserved sapwood (on right) from the Yarmouth Roads shipwreck (Isle of Wight, UK). Photographs by Sara Rich, © Maritime Archaeology, Ltd., 2016...28

Figure 19. Wedge sample removed from a slow-grown oak timber composing the wrecked eighteenth-century frigate *La Santa Maria Magdalena* (Galicia, Spain). Photographs by Sara Rich, © Maritime Archaeology, Ltd., 2015 29

Figure 20. Timber sample record sheet produced on a Samsung Galaxy Note Pro 12.2 tablet 32

Figure 21. Method for storing samples that protects and keeps the wood wet but reduces exposure to aerobic bacterial and fungal agents. Drawings © Sara Rich, 2017..35

Figure 22. 2D image of the 3D site model produced through photogrammetry of the wrecked sixteenth-century galleon at Ribadeo (Galicia, Spain), hosted on Sketchfab. Model by Brandon Mason, ©Maritime Archaeology Ltd., 2015 46

Figure 23. Example of an inter- and multi-disciplinary work flow, as modeled by the ForSEAdiscovery project, which aims to elucidate Iberian timber trade for shipbuilding and the effects of shipbuilding on deforestation in the peninsula during the Age of Discovery. Image © Ana Crespo Solana 48

Acknowledgements

The production of this document has been initiated and supported by ForSEAdiscovery: Forest Resources for Iberian Empires – Ecology and Globalization in the Age of Discovery (Marie Curie Actions Programme PITN-2013-GA607545). The authors thanks the project fellows and partners for invaluable discussions and for reading and commenting on drafts. This document has also benefited greatly from insights and advice offered by staff members of Maritime Archaeology Trust and its trading partner Maritime Archaeology Ltd. Other assistance and insights have been provided by the Maritime Archaeology Research Lab of the University of Cyprus and its director, Stella Demesticha.

Chapter 1
The Uniquely Problematic Shipwrecks of the Equally Problematic 'Age of Discovery'

Two of the questions most frequently asked by archaeologists of sites and the objects that populate them are 'How old are you?' and 'Where are you from?' These questions can often be answered through **archaeometric** dating and provenance analyses. As both archaeological sites and objects, shipwrecks pose a special problem in archaeometric dating and provenance because when they sailed, they often accumulated new construction material as timbers were repaired and replaced. Additionally, during periods of globalization, such as the so-called Age of Discovery, the provenance of construction materials may not reflect where the ship was built due to long-distance timber trade networks and the global nature of these ships' sailing routes. Accepting these special challenges, **nautical archaeologists** must piece together the nuanced relationship between the ship, its timbers, and the shipwreck, and to do so, wood samples must be removed from the assemblage. Besides the provenance of the vessel's wooden components, selective removal and analysis of timber samples can also provide researchers with unique insights relating to **environmental history**. For this period, wood samples could help produce information on the emergent global economy; networks of timber trade; forestry and carpentry practices; climate patterns and anomalies; forest reconstruction; repairs made to ships and when, why, and where those occurred; and much more.

This book is a set of protocols to establish the need for wood samples from shipwrecks and to guide archaeologists in the removal of samples for a suite of **archaeometric** techniques currently available to provenance the timbers used to construct wooden ships and boats. While these protocols will prove helpful to archaeologists working on shipwreck assemblages from any time period and in any place, this book uses Iberian ships of the 16th to 18th centuries as its case studies because their global mobility poses additional challenges to the problem at hand (see below 1.3 and 2). At the same time, their prolificacy and ubiquity make the wreckage of these ships a uniquely global phenomenon.

Beginning with a brief historical overview of these vessels' place in Early Modern history, this guide also highlights some characteristics that are thought to be unique to ships of the Iberian-Atlantic shipbuilding tradition during this period, and which could make these vessels easier to identify *in situ*. However, the primary aim is to provide archaeological researchers with a set of protocols as to when and why *in-situ* timber sampling may be called for, how to go about it, and what to do with the samples afterward (for sampling *ex situ*, see Orton 2000, 191-209). A disclaimer should be stated, though, that perusing this guide will not qualify the reader as a specialist in either nautical archaeology or wood science; instead, specialist assistance should always be sought while conducting fieldwork, and ideally, before excavation even begins (Nayling in Coles & Goodburn 1991). In its educational capacity, this set of protocols is meant to complement and supplement existing guidelines on shipwreck excavation (Bowens 2009; Historic England 2015d [2010b]), dendrochronological sampling (Domínguez-Delmás et al. in prep, b; Brewer & Jansma 2016; Historic England 2015a [1998]), and handling waterlogged wooden artefacts (Historic England 2015c [2010a]).

1.1. Historical Background

Contemporary nautical construction is such a continuous, global occurrence that rarely if ever do we consider where container ships, oil tankers, or cruise ships were constructed; not even the construction of naval vessels can be taken for granted to have occurred in the nation they represent (Gordon 2015). In an era of unprecedented globalization, it is sometimes difficult to imagine our world without interconnections that circumnavigate the planet. Being a highly mobile species, the roots of complex trade networks and global colonization are nearly as old as are humans, but the foundations of consistently global mobility were established in the Age of Discovery, during the 16th to 18th centuries (Giraldez 2015; Crespo Solana 2012; Polónia & Barros 2012).

Also, and arguably more accurately, called the Age of Exploration, Age of Sail, Age of Empire, and Age of Trade, this period was characterized by a rapidly changing and complex political landscape; new perspectives on land, sea, and people, along with the ownership thereof; and a gradual awareness that the landmasses of the earth are little more than vast islands sharing a single body of water. Even at the beginning of the colonial race, Spanish and Portuguese sailing vessels were already plying the earth's waterways to establish empires that spanned multiple hemispheres, eastern and western, northern and southern.

These unprecedented imperial ventures contributed to the movement of ideas and ideologies (religions, languages, technologies, politics), animals, plants and pathogens; and people both free and enslaved. The desire to develop and dominate transoceanic pathways was fueled by trade in spices and slaves, but these quests also had a strong religious component. Between the Reconquista (1492) and the Ottoman defeat at the Battle of Lepanto (1571), anti-Islamic religious sentiment in Iberia mandated that Christian forces reach East Asia before the great Islamic empires – Ottoman, Safavid and Mughal – beat them to it (Hamdani 1997; Noonan 2007; Matar 1999; Kelsey 2016; Casale 2010). So in the same spirit of the Crusades or the Reconquista, the Christian crowns of Spain and Portugal conquered, converted, and controlled territory dispersed across five different continents: North and South America, Europe, Africa, and Asia.

Iberian maritime expansion and the parallel development of a naval industry also had a global impact due to the widespread and rapid transfer of technical and technological knowledge. Changes to traditional ship construction to better facilitate oceanic voyages were necessitated by the exploitation of trade winds that opened up the Atlantic, linking Iberia with the Canaries and Azores, and then with the Lesser Antilles, and finally, the whole of the Caribbean Sea and Gulf of Mexico (Figure 1; Crespo Solana 2014). Soon afterward, Africa, Asia, and the rest of the Americas were irreversibly inducted into the greater Atlantic social environment.

Almost immediately after Columbus made landfall in Hispaniola and returned to Castile, Spain and Portugal realized that they were each other's primary competition. The competing monarchies compromised and signed treaties that redistributed newly 'discovered' (albeit already inhabited) lands between them. The Treaty of Tordesillas (1494) set a line of demarcation in the Atlantic dictating that what lay to the west (most of the Americas) belonged to Spain and what lay to the east (including Brazil, the Azores, and Africa) belonged to Portugal (Waisberg 2017; Coben 2015). When disputes began in the South Pacific, the Treaty of Zaragoza (1529) added another demarcating line that gave the East Indies to Portugal and the Pacific Ocean to Spain, although by 1565, Spain would breach that meridian to claim the Philippines for itself (Hayes 2001; Giraldez 2015; Kelsey 2016). The efficacy of these treaties and the demarcations they intimated were often disputed, and the Church frequently intervened. However, the Protestant explorers to the north, namely English and Dutch, like the Muslim Ottomans to the east, disregarded the border allocations altogether, as the Pope had no legitimate control over their seafaring endeavors. As such, much of the European land race was conducted over water. This fact lead to ambitious shipbuilding regimes, swapping of trade secrets, and rapid changes to traditional ship architecture. Inevitably, it also means that the wreckage of ships of European and especially Iberian-Atlantic shipbuilding traditions are found in waterways the world over (Castro 2005, Appendix B; Isorena 2015; Giraldez 2015; Kelsey 2016).

Populating the length of the *Carrera de las Indias* between Spain and the Americas, the *Carreira da Índia* between Lisbon (Portugal) and Goa (India), and the Manila Galleon trade route between Manila (Philippines) and Acapulco (Mexico) are hundreds of Iberian shipwrecks known and unknown, whose

Chapter 1 The Uniquely Problematic Shipwrecks of the Equally Problematic 'Age of Discovery'

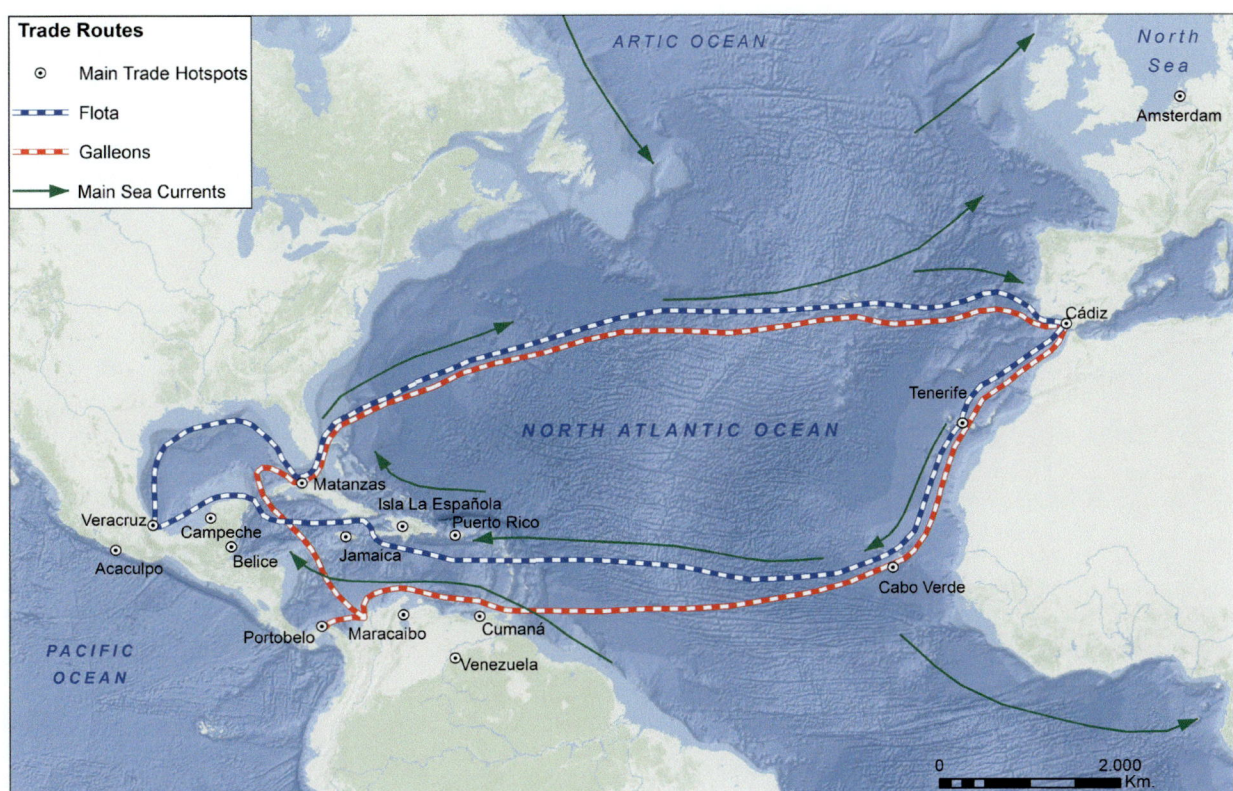

Service Layer Credits: Esri, DeLorme, GEBCO, NOAA NGDC, and other contributors
Author: María José García Rodríguez. ForSEADiscovery Project.

Figure 1. Map of main North Atlantic ocean currents, corresponding with trade winds and Iberian trans-Atlantic sailing routes from the late 15th century. Map prepared by María José García Rodríguez with data from Ana Crespo Solana, © ForSEAdiscovery Project, 2016.

trade ambitions connected Iberia to areas far beyond its direct control (Figure 2; Crespo Solana 2011). Their individual and collective stories narrate the history and origins of the modern world, and yet we still know relatively little about them (Gordon 2015).

1.2. Emergent oceangoing ship types

The origins of Renaissance-period ship design are still under debate by nautical archaeologists and maritime historians. There are three main lines of thought: 1) Mediterranean carvel-built ships spread into the Atlantic in the 15th century, 2) Spanish and Portuguese shipwrights were more influenced by English and Nordic traditions even before the advent of carvel planking, or 3) the geographical location of the Iberian peninsula made it a confluence of ship design and construction practices hailing from both the Mediterranean and the North Seas, along with Arab influences (Steffy 2001; Loewen 1998; Phillips 1986; Martin 2000; Castro 2005; Castro 2008; Agius 2008; Loureiro 2012; Casabán 2017).

There are three main types of oceangoing ship in use during this period in Iberia, each with its own set of functions and qualities, although these could and did often overlap. These ships are all hybrid forms, and at the time of writing, the form best attested in the archaeological record is the galleon (Vivas Pinedas 1998; Phillips 1986). Only one *nau*, the Portuguese Indiaman known as the Pepper Wreck, has been identified and excavated (Castro 2005). Other carracks and caravels *may* be attested at various sites around the world (Figure 2; see Castro 2005, Appendix B; the early sixteenth-century date and proportions of the Highbourne Cay wreck (Bahamas) suggests that it may be one of these two ship

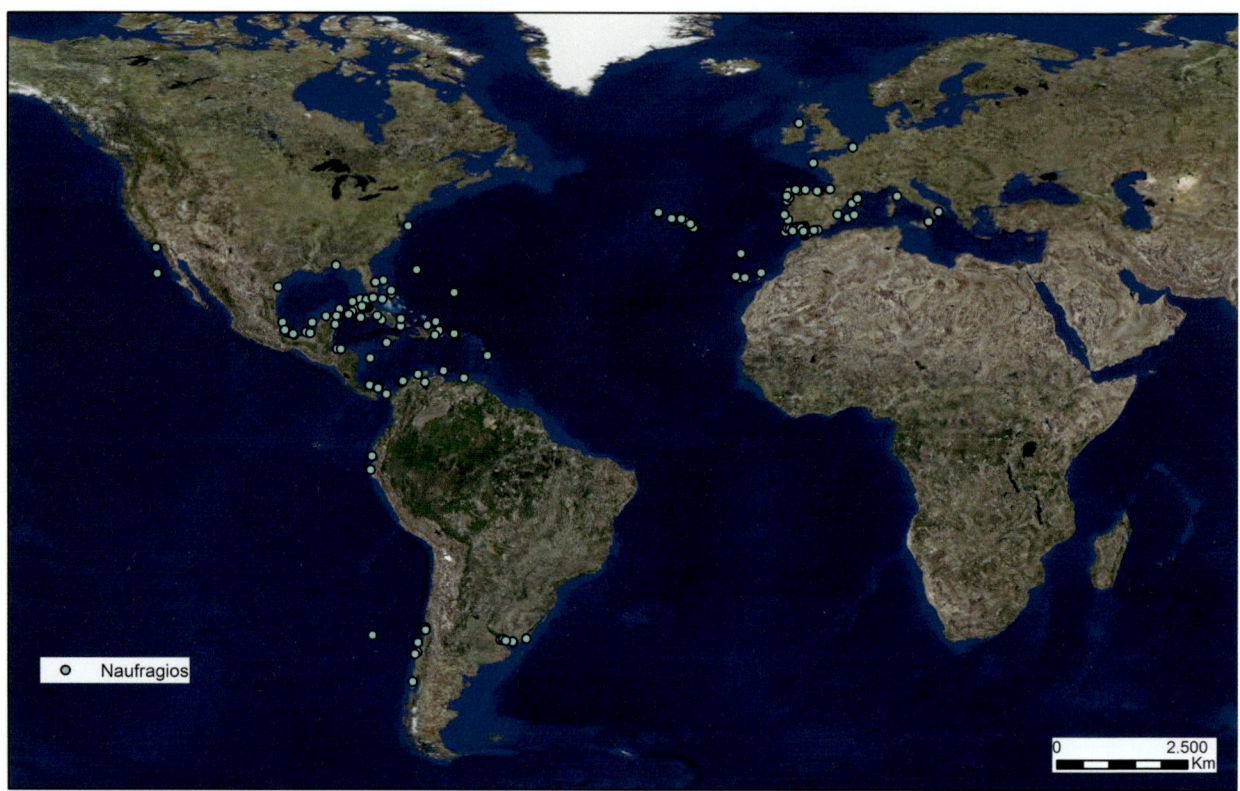

Figure 2. Distribution map of known sixteenth to eighteenth-century Iberian shipwrecks in the Atlantic Ocean and the Pacific coast of the Americas. Of these, 698 are known from historical records and 216 from archaeological investigations. The western Pacific and Indian Oceans surely harbor comparable numbers of vessels, although fewer have been identified and investigated as of yet. The Global Shipwrecks Database, from which this map was produced, seeks to continually build upon its existing dataset and incorporate other databases of Iberian shipwreck sites around the world. Map prepared by María José García Rodríguez with data from Ana Crespo Solana, © ForSEAdiscovery Project, 2016.

types: Smith et al. 1985; Oertling 1989), but the caravel is at this time only attested in iconographical and historical archives. Furthermore, it seems that at times, the Iberian term *nao* or *nau* was synonymous with the pan-European forms of the carrack and even caravel (Castro 2008; Flatman 2009; Phillips 1986). As state-sponsored experiments with hybrid forms continued, the galleon and the carrack also merged into a single unit capable of both war and trade; indeed even those two opposing aspects of cross-cultural contact were little more than two sides of the same Piece of Eight (Gordon 2015; Phillips 1986).

1.2.1. Galleon

The main function of galleons was in battle; however they also had commercial functions as they carried valuable cargoes and protected the rest of the merchant fleet. They feature two or three decks; a low-set fore and a higher aft castle; three or four masts and a bowsprit using both square (fore, main, and bowsprit) and lateen (mizzen and fourth mast, or 'bonaventure') sails (Martin 2000; Castro 2005; Casabán 2017; Phillips 1986). Probably developing out of Mediterranean galleys, galleons were longer than carracks and *naos*, with an average length to breadth proportion of 4:1, which decreased water resistance and increased maneuverability. They featured a square stern which supported the higher aft castle and allowed for more deck space and mounted cannons, which were evenly distributed around the hull (Phillips 1986).

1.2.2. Nao, nau, carrack

Nao (in Spanish) and *nau* (in Portuguese) are generic words for 'ship' but, along with 'carrack' (from Italian *caracca*), they typically refer to a vessel with between two and four decks; well integrated fore and aft castles; and three or four masts, of which the mizzenmast and bonaventure bore lateen sails, with the other one or two bearing square sails (Castro 2005; Phillips 1986). From iconography, the stern of a carrack can be square or round, and its proportions are typical of Mediterranean round ships at 3:1 length to breadth. These vessels could be enormous in size and had an alleged carrying capacity of 500 to 600 tons, which facilitated long voyages to India or the Americas. Their average burden though was around 100 metric tons, doubling from the 16th to 17th century. Although their primary function was as merchantmen, sixteenth-century commentators said that a capacity of 400 tons would allow the vessel to be effective both in commerce and war. Fleets of merchantmen were always armed and were requisitioned by the navy when needed (Phillips 1986).

1.2.3. Caravel

The caravel developed out of an older Mediterranean prototype (compare *carabus* in Latin, κάραβος [karavos] in Greek, and قارب [qaarib] in Arabic) and was adapted in sixteenth-century Iberia to suit the needs of the *armada*. It typically featured four masts with all but the foremast supporting lateen sails. With a length to breadth ratio of 3.5:1, they were lightweight (about 50 tons compared to the 100 tons of a carrack), fast, and readily maneuverable (Castro 2005; Phillips 1986). Because they were adapted to different sailing circumstances on the Mediterranean and Atlantic coasts, and because of the ship type's antiquity and regional evolution, its telltale characteristics, even its favoring of lateen sails, change from place to place and time to time, rendering it perhaps more difficult to identify in the archaeological record than the other two ship types. From the iconographical record, by the 16th century, caravels may have morphed into a something similar to galleons in shape and silhouette (Castro 2005; Casabán 2017; Phillips 1986). However sparse the evidence in the archaeological record, the caravel is noted in historical sources as the ship of choice from the 15th to 17th centuries, after which its design and function apparently merged into either the carrack for commercial pursuits or the galleon for combat (Phillips 1986).

1.3. What it means to be 'Iberian'

The idea of an Iberian shipbuilding tradition is a modern descriptor constructed to categorize the origins of wrecked vessels. Those involved in the design and construction of ships during this period would likely not have thought of themselves as Iberian or Atlantic, or their methods as falling into these categories either. However, there are three different ways in which a ship or shipwreck might receive the qualifier 'Iberian': 1) it was built within the confines of an Iberian empire; 2) it was constructed with timber from within the Iberian Peninsula; or 3) it conforms to Iberian ship architecture. Contemporaneous historical and iconographical accounts assert that oceangoing vessels hailing from the Iberian peninsula shared a few common features: they were built empirically without architectural plans (at least until the mid-16th century); their designs were based on proportion and scale; and they were skeleton-first (frame-based), carvel-built with planks fixed flush to the frames (Castro 2005; Apestegui 1998). Recently, several archaeologists have compiled more detailed lists of characteristics that are common to the hulls of ships built along the Iberian coast, or elsewhere complying with what can be considered the same architectural tradition (compiled from Loewen 1998; Castro 2008; Oertling 2001; Loureiro 2012; see also Phillips 1986).

1. Deciduous oak (*Quercus* subg. *quercus* L.) dominates the structural timbers (frames, ceiling, decks, keel, etc.) as well as the treenails, although pine (*Pinus* spp. L.) may be used in the hull planking. Repaired or replaced timbers have been documented as chestnut (*Castanea sativa* Mill.), and other broadleaf woods have been noted in small quantities. The wood may be of inferior quality.

2. Oak **treenails** (25mm diameter) and iron fastenings (10-12mm square section) are both used in the hull, and at each join of a frame and a plank, two of each are used. Treenails may be composed of wood from roots.
3. Timber measures, or **scantlings**, are uniform, even between large and small ships:
   - floor timbers = 19-20cm square section
   - futtock square sections decrease from 19-20cm to 14cm at the upper deck
   - hull planks = 33-38cm wide, 4.5-6cm thick, and max. 10-11m long
   - deck and wall planks = 17-19cm wide, 3-3.5cm thick, and max. 10-11m long
4. Some first futtocks and floors are assembled laterally with dovetail mortise and tenon joints, forming pre-erected design frames. These alternate with 'floating futtocks' that are only fastened to the hull planks.
5. The notched keelson swells in size at the main mast step and is buttressed on each side against the bilge clamps (or footwale), and on one or both sides of the keelson, there is a semi-circular cavity in the wood that held the pump.
6. The outermost stringers, called *albaolas,* are crenelated and feature small inserted 'filler' planks, which seal the bilges.
7. Central frames are predesigned and preassembled.
8. Curved timbers (*couces*) connect the stem and sternpost. These are supported by a curved knee, over which is a y-shaped frame (*pica*) connected to the *couce* by deadwood (*coral*).
9. The transom is flat with a tall, more-or-less vertical sternpost.

While any one of these characteristics could be seen in a vessel of a different origin, when taken together, they are assumed to be diagnostic of pan-Iberian shipbuilding traditions from the 16th to 18th centuries. This method of identification is not without its problems: namely, that the sample of shipwrecks confirming these traits may have been engaged in Iberian trade, but it cannot be confirmed that all of them were built in Iberia, or by Iberians, or even necessarily for Iberians. Furthermore, there are many regional variations that may reflect outside influences (as in labor force or other technology transference mechanisms) or local specializations (construction of oceangoing versus estuarine vessels, or galleons versus caravels, e.g.) (Loureiro 2012). These ambiguities help make the case for why advancing the methods and analytical potentials of wood provenance is so important. If a broad sample of structural timbers could be dated and provenanced, it would elucidate the continuum – temporal and spatial – of the historical 'place' of the ship and all that went into making it and sailing it.

1.4. Treasure and archaeology

All shipwrecks are treasure troves of information, but few contain actual treasure. With romantic ideas of sunken hordes of gold doubloons and treasure chests of jewels guarded by one-eyed pirate skeletons, Spanish and Portuguese shipwrecks are especially vulnerable to the efforts of those who seek to profit financially, not culturally, from 'excavating' shipwrecks (e.g., Smith et al., 1985; Keith & Simmons III 1985). The practices of modern-day treasure hunters (who variously refer to themselves as salvors, explorers, or even commercial archaeologists) destroy heritage sites just to get to 'the rich stuff' (a phrase made famous in Steven Spielberg's 1985 film, *The Goonies*). The shipwreck assemblage is rarely if ever recorded, and excavations are less than systematic, let alone scientific. Neither are treasure hunters concerned with the socio-historical context of the gold and silver from which they hope to profit; namely, that it was mined by enslaved indigenous people whose torture was legitimized by the colonialist concepts of biological, cultural, and religious superiority (Beuchot 1997). Instead, artefacts 'salvaged' from such sites are sold to private collectors for profit, where, far more often than not, they disappear once again from public access and from the infinite lessons history has to teach us.

Archaeologists, in strict opposition to treasure hunters or 'salvage' teams, operate by way of a professional deontological code, or duty-based ethics (Brodie et al., 2006; Brodie & Tubb 2002; Castro, n.d.). **Deontology**, as it relates to cultural heritage, champions the production of knowledge over the production of profit because only the production of knowledge leads to the formulation of truths (see also Chapter 5). Those few archaeologists who are willing to collaborate with treasure hunters compromise their professional ethical code because even well-intended collaborations do not result in some idealized win-win situation. Instead, there will always be a conflict of interest (Juvelier 2017; Dromgoole 2002). All too often, shipwreck sites are excavated without being guided by research questions; they are inadequately mapped and documented; and any results (including the presence of decontextualized finds) are disseminated exclusively through popular media channels, eschewing scientific peer-reviewed publication altogether (e.g., Pope 2007; Butterfields 2000; Mathewson 1986; but see: Lu and Zhou 2016; Flecker 2002). Just as dangerously, the archaeological record becomes biased toward shipwrecks that have the potential to turn the most profit. It should be clear that all of these factors hinder the production of knowledge and truth. Legitimate archaeological organizations around the world have developed ethical codes of conduct, and financial gain from stolen and/or decontextualized tangible heritage is unanimously rejected (e.g., CifA 2014; see also http://worldarch.org/code-of-ethics/). The 2001 UNESCO Convention on the Protection of the Underwater Cultural Heritage (UCH) Article 2.7 states explicitly: 'Underwater cultural heritage shall not be commercially exploited' (full text available at www.unesco.org).

Not surprisingly, ship timbers do not usually promise a great deal of profit for treasure hunters, so they are forcefully removed or otherwise ruined in the search for more valuable artefacts. That being said, a large timber was recently found as flotsam on the coast of one of the Hebrides (Scotland), and in 2015, it was posted for sale on the online auction site Ebay with a starting bid of 750 GBP (Figure 3). The seller

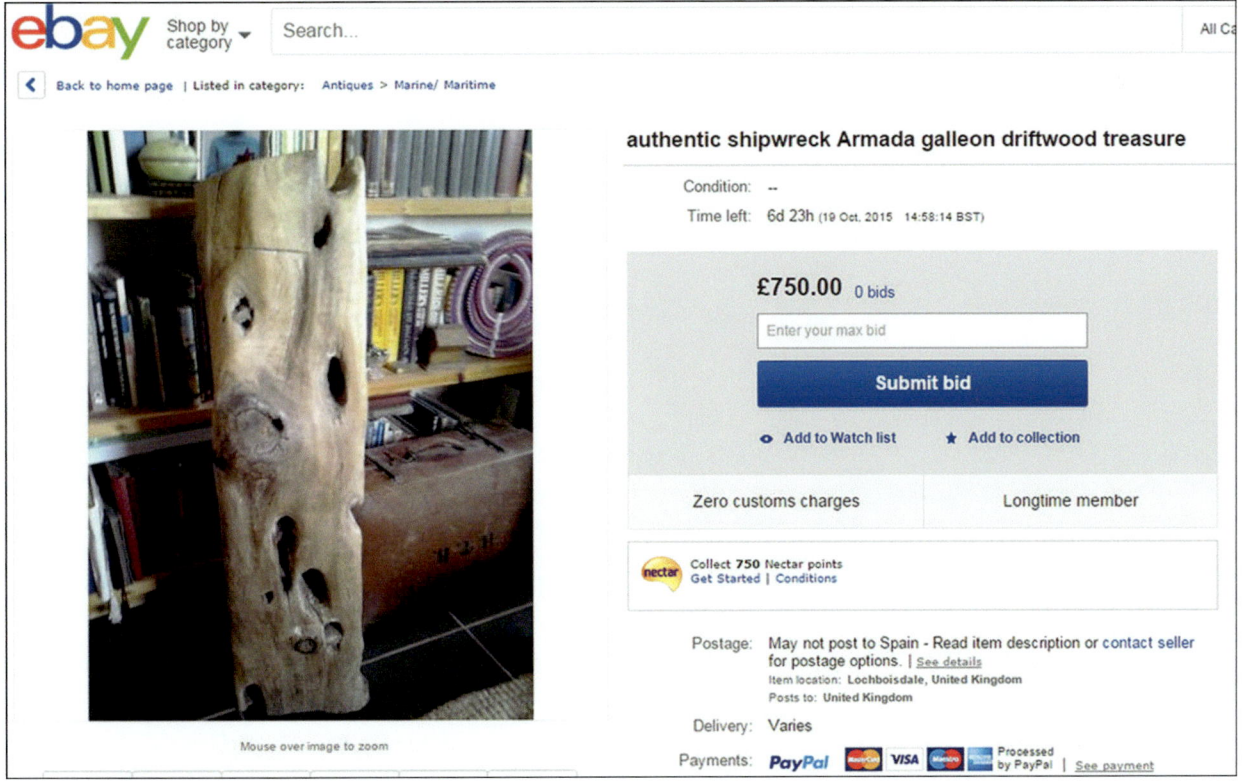

FIGURE 3. SUPPOSED SHIPWRECK TIMBER FROM A GALLEON OF THE 1986 SPANISH *ARMADA* THAT APPEARED ON THE ONLINE AUCTION SITE EBAY IN 2015 AFTER HAVING WASHED UP ON THE SCOTTISH COAST AS FLOTSAM.

described it as coming from one of Philip II's *armada* galleons wrecked in the storm of 1588 (Birch & McElvogue 1999; Martin 2000; Casabán 2017). Without context though, this claim cannot be validated, and it is unlikely that any archaeological project or wood science lab would be in a position (financially or ethically) to purchase the timber in order to confirm a date or origin (Huysecom et al. 2017). Whether a timber is destroyed or sold, either way, its scientific potential and historical relevance are irreversibly compromised in exchange for profit.

Online auction houses like Ebay are perfect vehicles for the global illicit trade in tangible cultural heritage, some of which supports the work of international terrorist organizations. While undoubtedly a global phenomenon, developing countries and areas experiencing armed conflict or regime change are most highly susceptible to looting and antiquities trafficking (Huysecom et al. 2017; Brodie et al. 2006; Flecker 2002). At the same time, collectors buying these stolen antiquities are most often found in the wealthiest and most politically stable countries, specifically the United States and the United Kingdom, where cultural artefacts devoid of their original context are demoted further to prestige badges and conversation pieces. This all too common scenario only serves to uphold colonialist conventions of the disempowered Other, as well as that of a present that is unnecessarily disarticulated from the past (Brodie et al. 2006; Lucas 2001, 2012).

Countries that have ratified the 2001 UNESCO convention on UCH may prosecute treasure hunters (O'Keefe 2013; Guérin & Egger 2010; Dromgoole 2002; for more on the UNESCO convention, see 5.1); however, in countries that have not yet ratified the convention, these individuals and companies may be paid handsomely for their crimes (often because they are not actually defined as such). It is worth emphasizing, however, that the profit is one-sided; in many cases, the costs of judicial proceedings and litigation resulting from contested activities or rights is publicly funded: that is, by the same taxpayers who will no longer have access to heritage items sold into private collections (Throckmorton 1998).

Chapter 2
Timber Samples and Dendroprovenance

While we often speak of find-spots in archaeology, original provenance is just as important to compiling an understanding of an object's place in history. When discussing dates of objects, there are often two: one for the construction and one for the deposition. Similarly, with highly mobile objects like ships, there are typically two locations because the place of deposition is not usually the same as the place of construction. Knowing both ends of the temporal and spatial spectra of an object helps us to trace what happened between these events, thereby becoming better equipped to answer questions related to mobility, interconnectivity, and resource acquisition and management (Crespo Solana 2015; Wing 2015; Loureiro 2012; Loewen 2000; de Aranda y Antón 1990, 1992; Guilló 1989). While cargo, personal belongings of the crew, and other items related to the ship's everyday functioning can be highly informative, to reveal the circumstances surrounding where a ship originated, it is necessary to examine the wood from which it was built.

In the study of ancient watercraft, wood could be considered the material of most fundamental interest. Historical records since Antiquity describe shipbuilding and mention the trees felled to furnish timbers for new vessels or even new navies. However, the implications of these texts depend on accurate translations of the flora listed, as well as accurate correlations between ancient toponyms and modern geographical features. Both of these tasks are notoriously problematic and are often contested by historians (e.g., Meiggs 1982). Archival information can also occasionally be misleading, as authors had their own agendas when writing, which may skew reality. The same is true for art historical sources. Therefore, archaeological sciences open up a complementary avenue for deriving this information from primary sources.

Wood can survive into the archaeological record in anaerobic environments that repel **xylophagic** organisms (Blanchette et al. 1990). Underwater, wood may be protected from wood-boring teredo (*Teredo navalis* L.), gribble (Limnoriidae White, 1850), and piddock (Pholadidae Lamarck, 1809) by lying beneath layers of mud or peat, for example (Palma & Santhakumaran 2014; Wilson 1993). Large wooden watercraft can also be preserved in intertidal zones or in rivers, frequently those that have been infilled with sediments (e.g., Nayling & Susperregi 2014). Several Iberian ships located around the world have been preserved through these exceptional depositional circumstances. And in the frequent absence of primary source texts like a ship's manifest, or archival records related to the vessel's construction, one way to determine its provenance is to consider the actual timbers from which it was fashioned. This approach is called **dendroprovenance**, and several methods have been developed to achieve it, each with its own set of potentials and limitations.

Determining the provenance of shipwrecks is a notoriously tricky issue due to multi-culturalism inherent in the maritime world (cf. Harpster 2013; Casale 2007). Cargo is traced to various ports of call, as are crew members and passengers, and even the ones building or designing the ship may be foreign to the dockyard where it was constructed. To make matters even hazier, a ship may have been built at one locale and purchased or commandeered at another, or owned by a person of one ethnicity and operated by another (Ahlström 1997; Casale 2007; Phillips 1986, 20). Therefore, while questions of ship ethnicity may lead only to dead ends, pursuing questions of its provenance can lead to fruitful discussions of resource acquisition, timber trade, timber transport, and the relationships between forestry (and often, deforestation) and shipyard activities, not to mention valuable information about types and qualities of wood and their function and efficacy as ship timbers (Figure 4; Wing 2015; Loureiro 2012; Loewen 2001; Loewen & Delhaye 2006; Phillips 1986).

> **POSSIBLE RESEARCH QUESTIONS FOR INTERROGATING SHIP TIMBERS**
>
> - What species of trees were used in the ship's construction?
> - From where did these trees originate?
> - How could one characterize the distribution of old to juvenile trees used in the ship's construction?
> - Did the trees originate from a managed forest? If so, who managed it and why?
> - Were multiple timbers converted from the same tree?
> - Which conversion methods were used for which timbers and why?
> - If trees for construction originated from disparate regions, what can be deduced about timber trade, the location and date of the ship's construction, repairs made to the ship (and why those occurred)?
> - Can the growth patterns of the parent trees be extrapolated by examining those present in the timbers?
> - How did shipwrights and carpenters access and convert trees into ship timbers?
> - What were some of the shipwright's decision-making processes that went into the architecture of this ship?
> - Did the shipwright conform to the norms of ship construction for his time and place?
> - Do the timbers betray the circumstances leading up to the wrecking event?
> - How stable is the timber assemblage in the wake of destructive bio-, geo-, and anthropogenic forces?

FIGURE 4. EXAMPLES OF RESEARCH QUESTIONS THAT COULD FORM THE BASIS FOR INTERROGATING A WOODEN SHIPWRECK SITE THROUGH A SYSTEMATIC TIMBER SAMPLING CAMPAIGN.

The development of extensive timber trade networks, however, brings up another potential stumbling block in efforts at provenancing a vessel's place of construction via its wood. Even if a ship's timbers can be provenanced to a specific region, that does not necessarily mean that the vessel was built at the nearest shipyard; it only indicates the origin of the wood. In theory, the timber could have been transported to any number of distant shipyards and the vessel constructed there. However, recent provenance studies performed on ship timbers have determined that Northern and Western European shipyards relied most heavily on nearby forests, so the provenance of ship timbers was indicative of the provenance of the ship (see Jensen et al. in Crumlin-Pedersen & Olsen 2002; Daly 2007, 229, 236-237; Allevato et al. 2009). On the other hand, there are exceptions, even within a Northern European context (Bridge 2011), especially with regards to ships constructed of imported southern Baltic oak, a common scenario from the 13th to 19th centuries (Wazny 2005; Daly & Nymoen 2008; Vermeersch & Haneca 2015; Vermeersch et al. 2015).

The massive 30m-long ships built during the Age of Discovery were constructed of thousands of trees. Oak was still the primary ship timber, but pine, chestnut, elm, and others were used as well. In Iberian shipbuilding, it is known that at least some of the timbers originated from local forests. For example, historical data from the Basque Country indicates that forest reserves along the coastal frontier were designated for the naval shipyards; at the same time, other timbers were imported from the Baltic and beyond (Wing 2015; Ruano 2013; Loewen 2000; de Aranda y Antón 1992; Gallagher 2016; Trindade et al., in prep; Phillips 1986; for Portuguese naval forests, see: Monchet & Santos 2015; Loureiro 2012). With forest reserves and imports monopolized by the financial and political elites, who gravitated around the imperial ruling circles, patterns of species distribution and growth conditions were increasingly imposed through management upon the forest geography of Iberia and the empires. Even with the existing historical and archaeological knowledge bases, it is not possible to arrive at a complete and accurate understanding of these patterns without the assistance of dendrochronology and other types of wood characterization studies (Crespo Solana & Nayling 2016).

Even if knowing the origin of a single piece of wood will not rewrite the history of shipbuilding or naval forestry, **dendroprovenance** techniques can still be used to fill in the gaps of what we do know about the vessel: where it's been and when. In turn, this information can contribute to a better understanding of historical landscapes and maritime industry. It can provide scientific credence (or revoke it) for assumptions made from historical data: e.g., in Iberia, that extensive shipbuilding was largely responsible for deforestation, despite accusations from the crown that Italian and Dalmatian immigrants bore the culpability; that shipwrights followed architectural treatises and proscriptive ordinances for constructing ships; or that wood was harvested during winter months on days with a waning moon (Phillips 1986). Essentially, a timber sample is not just a piece of soggy old wood; it is a unique archival dataset that bears a great responsibility for representing the timber, the ship, the seas it sailed, and the forest whence it came (cf. Loewen 2000; Goodburn in Coles & Goodburn 1991).

2.1. Scientific analyses

Wood origin has been the focus of numerous of scientific investigations in recent years, stemming from advances in dendrochronology and wood characterization studies, and realizing the potentials and limitations of each (Eckstein & Wrobel 2007; Bridge 2012; Domínguez-Delmás 2013). In response, new scientific methods have been developed and old ones adapted to address common historical assumptions and the general lack of accurate information about anthropogenic fluctuations in world forests. These methods were also advanced to better understand alterations in species distribution and the complexities of trade networks. Current lab-based **dendroprovenance** techniques include dendrochronology, dendroarchaeology, DNA studies, trace element and isotopic analyses, and anatomical/structural markers (Figure 5). Each of these methods is consistently being further developed and improved so that the current range of applications can be expanded temporally and spatially, and to include more wood types in varying conditions. Dendrochronology and dendroarchaeology are the two most cost-effective, but each analytical method comes with its own set of limitations and benefits, so ideally, multiple methods should be pursued for any given sample.

Analysis	What it looks for	What it can provide (best case scenario)	What the analyst needs (from each sample)	Possible to sub-sample or share between other analysts?	Condition of the sample
Dendroarchaeology	Taxa ID and overlapping range of distribution between identified elements; alt. macroscopic growth and conversion patterns	Identify types of wood used for different elements and possibly provenance	2-3cm³ with some annual growth rings along with tangential and radial sides; alt. full cross-section for growth and conversion patterns	Yes	If recovered from underwater, still waterlogged or post-conservation
Dendrochronology	Sequences of annual growth rings that align with master regional chronology	Identification of taxa used, felling date of parent tree, and provenance	Transverse section of stem with >80 annual growth rings; ideally sapwood and bark edge through pith	Yes	If recovered from underwater, still waterlogged or post-conservation; unbroken, ring boundaries visible and uninterrupted
DNA	Isolation and amplification of chloroplast DNA	Identification of taxa and genetic variations indicating growth environment: provenance	If dry and undamaged, 400mg; if wet and/or damaged by wood-borers, >1g	No – destructive analysis susceptible to contamination	Minimal contamination; kept in sterile container
Geochemistry	Elemental composition including trace elements and ratios of stable isotopes	Alignment with known forests with similar composition: provenance	50g of uncontaminated wood from stem or branch, or large enough that contaminated outer areas may be removed	Yes – destructive analysis may subsample after non-destructive analyses if no further contamination is introduced	Minimal contamination including during conservation processes; kept in sterile container
Organic chemistry	Patterns in molecular composition of carbohydrates, tannins, and resins and molecular bond vibrations of cellulose and lignin	Alignment with known forests of similar molecular composition and bond vibration patterns: provenance	15cm of transverse section including bark and pith if possible; 5cm radial and 5cm tangential sections of stem	Yes – destructive analysis may subsample after non-destructive analyses	If recovered from underwater, still waterlogged; minimal contamination including during conservation processes; kept in sterile container
Wood anatomy	Microscopic variations of cellular growth and growth anomalies	Align with topographical, geological, or environmental conditions producing such patterns or anomalies: provenance	>40 annual growth rings from transverse section of stem	Yes	If recovered from underwater, still waterlogged or post-conservation; unbroken, ring boundaries visible and uninterrupted

FIGURE 5. TABLE WITH DESCRIPTIONS OF ANALYTICAL DENDROPROVENANCE METHODS AND WHAT EACH REQUIRES FROM A WOOD SAMPLE.

2.1.1. Dendrochronology

While tree-ring signatures are a well-known method for dating archaeological wood, and as indicators for long-term regional climate change, dendrochronology can also be used for wood provenance. The method has been demonstrated frequently in nautical contexts using the regional oak chronologies of Northern Europe (e.g., Domínguez-Delmás et al., in prep, a; Bojakowski & Custer-Bojakowski 2017; Vermeersch & Haneca 2015; Vermeersch et al. 2015; Krąpiec & Krąpiec 2014; Haneca & Daly 2014; Domínguez-Delmás et al. 2013; Daly 2007; Daly & Nymoen 2008; Nayling & Susperregi 2014; Wazny 2011; Bridge 2011). Recent dendrochronological interrogations of ship and shipwreck assemblages in North America have also been successful (Creasman 2012; Creasman et al. 2015). Sequences of **annual growth rings** beginning with living trees are continually matched and extended further and further back into the past; at the same time, tree-ring sequences specific to certain growth areas may be unified, forming **master regional chronologies**. Corresponding regional idiosyncrasies in tree-ring signatures allow for unknown archaeological samples to be matched temporally and spatially, providing both a date and a provenance. However, in regions where no master regional chronology exists yet, such as Iberia, dendrochronology can still provide a date (often in conjunction with ^{14}**C wiggle matching**; see, e.g., Manning et al. 2014; Lorentzen et al. 2014), and other methods such as dendroarchaeology or anatomical markers can be used to suggest a provenance (Domínguez-Delmás et al. 2015; Domínguez-Delmás 2013). Tree ring databases (e.g., ITRDB) and existing chronologies are systematically being updated and modified, and it is expected that this method will continue to be exceedingly important for shipwreck archaeology in the future. This is one reason why all samples taken should be submitted to a dendrochronology lab so that they can be incorporated into existing chronologies, thereby strengthening the dataset and increasing its application and accuracy.

Wood from ships and wrecks may be characterized by material from several different regions (susceptible to different climate signals), of several different species (showing different climate-growth correlations), in varying levels of preservation, and in many cases, from coppiced woods or plantations (carrying a strong management signal); for this reason, wood from nautical origins alone cannot be used to construct regional chronologies (see Guibal & Pomey 2004; Wicha 2005; Bridge 2011). Instead, ring-width chronologies should be constructed from living trees overlapped with increasingly old heritage assets in the region, such as historic timber buildings and archaeological sites where the timber is likely to be of local origin. On the other hand, site masters (or object chronologies) are composed from individual shipwrecks (or any other individual site or object), which can be informative as to the characteristics of the wood used in the object's construction. Even if the site master cannot be cross-matched with any existing regional master chronologies, or even other site masters, it may eventually be **cross-dated** with a chronology that is yet to be developed (Domínguez-Delmás et al., in prep, b).

2.1.2. Dendroarchaeology

Dendroarchaeology relies on confirmed taxa IDs and distribution maps to determine the overlapping growth range of species represented in a given assemblage. This area of overlap is taken as the locale for construction, while the current distribution maps are assumed (relatively) unchanged from the past (e.g., Liphschitz 2007; 2009; 2012a, b). Taxonomists and palynologists may find this method's base assumptions problematic. First inter-genus and inter-species relationships and subdivisions thereof are not always agreed upon. Second, many trees cannot be identified to the species level based on visible microscopic characteristics alone (Schoch et al. 2004). For example, three widely distributed species of European oak (*Q. robur, Q. petraea, Q. pubescens*) commonly used in shipbuilding cannot be differentiated by wood anatomy, so dendroarchaeology alone would not be able to ID, let alone provenance, these woods (cf. Rich et al. 2016; Domínguez-Delmás et al., in prep, b). Third, **palynology** demonstrates that flora distribution fluctuated frequently in the past, as it does now (e.g., Sadori et al. 2013). These caveats aside, if the taxonomy is homogeneous and the geographical area of distribution is restricted, a possible provenance of the timbers and the shipyard can be inferred (Guibal & Pomey 2003). Moreover, dendroarchaeology can be helpful in supporting other provenance methods: for example, pollen analysis has been used in conjunction with dendroarchaeology to provenance shipwreck timbers and even delimit areas of possible ancient shipyards (Allevato et al. 2009; Muller 2005; Giachi et al. 2003). By itself, dendroarchaeology can also be used to provenance wood securely identified to the species level and dating to relatively recent periods that might better reflect current distribution patterns.

The next logical extension of the traditional methods and aims of provenance through taxonomy include more holistic approaches to macroscopic investigations. Timbers from the Highbourne Cay and Belinho shipwrecks have been identified as being constructed with immature European deciduous oak trees (*Quercus* subg. *quercus*) based on macro anatomical features, along with ring counts, average ring widths, and presence of **sapwood** and **waney edge** (see 3.1; Castro et al., 2015; Martins et al., in press). Dimensions of sampled **cross-sections** indicate **scantlings**, and sketches indicate conversion methods used in the shipyard (see 1.3). A compilation of this data can also be used to contribute to a hypothesis of the location of source forests and/or the location of the shipyard where the vessel was constructed.

2.1.3. DNA

In non-archaeological applications, **DNA barcoding** has isolated sources for modern tropical timbers to within 300m of where they were felled, which makes it a powerful method to track illegal timber trafficking in tropical regions (e.g., Jiao et al. 2014; and globaltimbertrackingnetwork.org). However, its archaeological application is debated because the **chloroplast DNA** (cpDNA) signal becomes obfuscated with the material's degradation, whether old and dry or waterlogged. That being said, archaeological poplar (*Populus euphratica* Oliv.) wood from China was amplified with PCR (**polymerase chain reaction**) and differentiated from others within the same genus (Jiao et al. 2015; see also Deguilloux et al. 2004; Dumolin-Lapègue et al. 1999). Exciting new advancements in PCR amplification resulted in the taxonomical identification of a broad array of ancient, long-lived trees (Gómez-Zeledón et al. 2017), which is equally encouraging for **maritime archaeological** applications of gene studies, although more experimentation remains necessary. From an underwater context, the cpDNA of one oak sample from the *Mary Rose* shipwreck (1510-1545) was successfully extracted (Speirs et al. 2009), which is again suggestive of the potential for (sub-)species identification, and therefore provenance, to be derived from aged, waterlogged wood (Borgin 1975).

2.1.4. Geochemistry

Mass spectrometry (using, e.g., ICP-MS, or an inductively-coupled mass spectrometer) can highlight the chemical or elemental relationship between specific geological environments and the trees that grow on them. Plants leach chemicals from the local bedrock, hydrology, and atmosphere, and measurements of these elemental or isotopic ratios in wood can be used to develop species- and location-specific isotopic or trace element spatial signatures. Primary **trace elements** examined are Ba, Mn, Cu, Zn, and Pb, and stable **isotopes** include $\delta^{18}O$, $\delta^{13}C$, $\delta^{15}N$, and the ratio of $^{87}Sr/^{86}Sr$. However, because accurate contributor proxies cannot be developed, and a 'map' can never really be complete, these techniques are limited to ruling out pre-existing hypotheses (Pollard 2011), which are usually based on other typologies (e.g., ceramic, numismatic), iconography, or textual references in contemporaneous literature (Rich 2016). For example, analyses of the ratios of certain isotopes of strontium ($^{87}Sr/^{86}Sr$) can be applied to archaeological wood to provide either a match or non-match between the archaeological sample and its supposed origin (Graustein & Armstrong 1983; Gosz & Moore 1989; Durand et al. 1999; English et al. 2001; Reynolds et al. 2005). By themselves, matches, even of identical isotopic ratios, cannot absolutely ensure a geographical origin though because the very same ratio could be found in a region that has not been sampled and for which no 'map' or spatial signature exists (Rich et al. 2012, 2015). So while this method offers a unique way to weed out pre-existing origin hypotheses, it is best coupled with other approaches, scientific or historical, to generate new hypotheses or modify old ones (e.g., Rich et al. 2016).

2.1.5. Anatomical and structural markers

Wood characterization studies that examine the anatomical anomalies and structural chemistry of a sample can be used to identify common growth habitats. For example, samples from Iberian forests known to have furnished ship timber are sampled, and these are analysed for microscopic and chemical tracers that indicate elevation, slope, soil acidity, hydration, frost, parasitic attacks, fire outbreaks, pollution exposure, etc. Trees from the same growth environment exhibit the same anomalies, so when archaeological wood is compared, it is possible to trace its provenance by matching these anomalies (somewhat similar to dendrochronological and geochemical techniques). **FTIR** measures molecular bond vibrations (especially of **cellulose** and **lignin**), and **Py-GC/MS** measures macromolecular compositions (such as **carbohydrates, tannins,** and **resins**) (Traoré et al. 2016; Khanjian et al. 2012; Chen et al. 2010; Łuceijko et al. 2009; Colombini et al. 2007); like other techniques described above, the combined results provide distinct 'signatures' based on species, habitat, and development.

Chapter 3
Sampling and Sub-sampling

While removing pieces of wood from a shipwreck may sound fairly straightforward, it is anything but. Every shipwreck is different, and its unique assemblage, location, condition, and preservation requirements must be taken into account before selecting timbers. Choosing the right timbers to represent the ship and its wreck, and to be of scientific value, is half the battle (Figure 6; Domínguez-Delmás et al., in prep, b; Nayling in Coles & Goodburn 1991). And these decisions will be made, generally, underwater. Once a timber has been sampled and brought to the surface, it is detached from the shipwreck assemblage, so recording all samples before and after they are taken is an essential part of maintaining the site archive (Marsden in Coles & Goodburn 1991; see 4.4). Furthermore, each scientific analysis has its own set of requirements for a sample, and often, compromises will have to be made to ensure both high quality **dendroprovenance** results and the integrity of the archaeological site (Figure 5; 3.3). It is expected that archaeology teams engaged in sampling procedures have sufficient experience and competence to carry out the work. This may involve consulting heritage agencies to recruit new team members experienced with waterlogged wood or wood science to assist or advise on the procedures described here. It could also mean providing the existing team with adequate training. No less than the cargo or personal items of the crew, ships and their timbers are invaluable components of material culture and should be treated with the same respect shown to other archaeological objects.

KEY CONSIDERATIONS WHEN DEVELOPING A TIMBER SAMPLING STRATEGY

- What information are you trying to obtain from the wood?
- Which analyses will be performed on the samples you take, and why?
- Who will be performing the analyses, and will a wood specialist be on site?
- What kinds of samples will the analyst(s) need? (number/type of rings, size of sample, number of samples, condition of wood, level of contamination tolerated, etc.)
- What is the condition of the shipwreck site?
- How will the condition of the shipwreck and the conditions of the site affect the number of samples taken?
- Which structural timbers will be targeted?
- How do those timbers selected represent the entire vessel?
- How will you ensure that the damage done to the vessel is minimized while the potential data to be gained from the samples is maximized?

Figure 6. Examples of questions to consider when developing an underwater timber sampling strategy.

As such, it should be emphasized first and foremost that when timbers are selected for potential sampling, they must be adequately recorded before inflicting any damage (ie., cutting or removing) on them. The second point of emphasis is that **sample populations** are not the same as **target populations** (Orton 2000, 181); in other words, when trying to understand the larger-scale construction contexts of, e.g., Iberian ships (target population), it is important to remember that the samples taken from a single shipwreck site (sample population) cannot be used to directly account for or explain the target with any precision. They can really only be representative of that shipwreck assemblage; however, these representatives can be projected to expand (or create) datasets of dates, chronologies, **scantlings**, provenances, tool marks, technological changes, and the myriad other data that can be derived from ship timbers. These in turn can contribute to explaining or predicting characteristics of the target population.

3.1. Selection

Three basic guidelines should be considered when selecting timbers to sample (adapted from Oxley in Coles & Goodburn 1991; see also Domínguez-Delmás 2013, and Nayling in Coles & Goodburn 1991):

- There should be evidence that the sample will contain data providing valuable information about the past. Evidence could include: numerous narrow visible rings, an unusual type of wood, visible **sapwood** or **waney edge**, important structural timber, or an unusually high level of preservation.
- There must be a sound reason for collecting the material. Specific research questions should be formulated and clear objectives maintained.
- There should be a clear prospect that the material will be studied and a clear route for how the material will be transported from the site to the laboratory. Consultation with specialists should be established before excavation even begins.

Structural timbers, such as hull planks, beams, keel and keelson, and frames, should be targeted for **dendroprovenance** sampling. These timbers are more likely to be representative of the ship's original architecture, and will therefore be more diagnostic as to the ship type and theoretically, where it was built and when (Domínguez-Delmás et al., in prep, b; Domínguez-Delmás 2013). However, if the research questions are more concerned with the route it sailed, or the frequency and extent of the repairs it faced, then more ephemeral timbers should also be targeted. The sampling strategy must reflect the research questions being asked (Figures 4, 6).

Some aspects of the timber selection strategy can be developed with a basic knowledge of wood properties and of period shipbuilding. For example, if **deciduous** oak (*Quercus* subg. *quercus* L.) is likely to have been used in structural timbers (as is the case for 'Iberian' ships as well as Ottoman, British, Scandinavian, French, and Dutch vessels of the Medieval and Early Modern periods; cf. de Aranda y Antón 1999), it will be crucial to take samples from both frames and planks.

In developing a sampling strategy to include frames and planks, there are two reasons for archaeologists to regard the growth pattern of **deciduous** oak as it pertains to shipbuilding. The first reason is that the rings, divided by medullary rays extending outward from the **pith** (and vertically through the trunk, or stem), are often visible on exposed **transverse** ends of timbers, making it possible to identify an oak timber underwater, without removing a sample at all (Figures 7, 8; Schweingruber 2012). It can then be estimated whether the oak was slow or fast grown and which **dendroprovenance** analyses could be conducted on a sample from it (Figure 5; 3.3).

The second reason is that deciduous oak (unlike the shrubbier evergreen (or 'live') oaks also used in shipbuilding) is a ring-porous wood, which means that during spring, it develops large cells that

Figure 7. Slivers of transverse sections of pine (*Pinus* sp.; left) and deciduous oak (*Quercus* subg. *Quercus*; right), demonstrating the visible differentiating features: color, sharper distinctions between annual growth rings in pine, porous earlywood in oak, and medullary rays in oak. Photograph © Sara Rich, 2017.

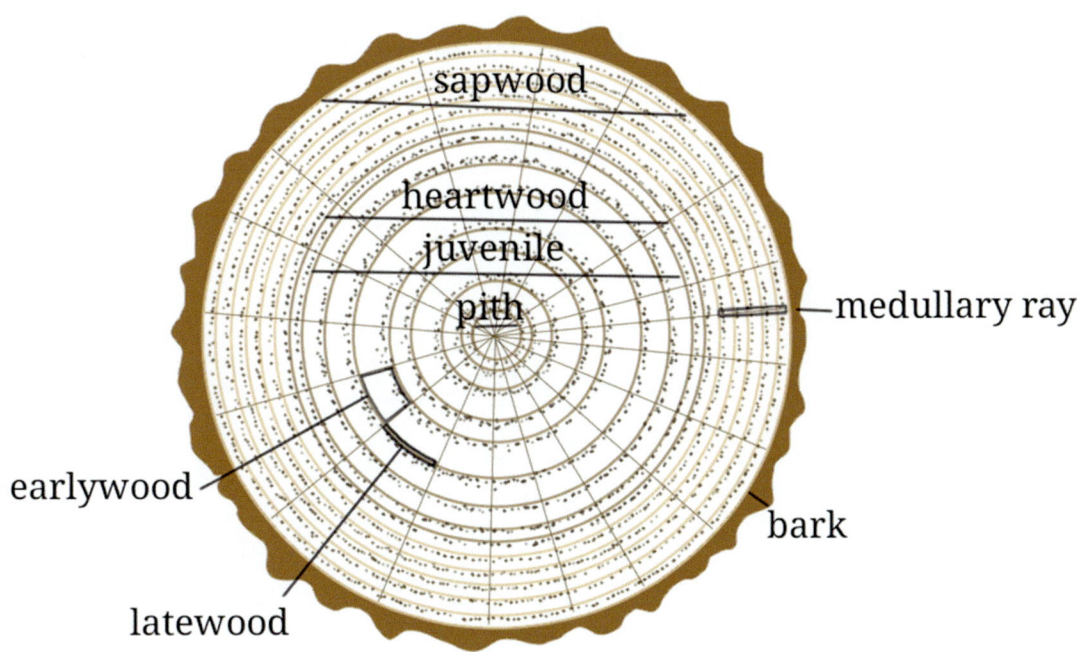

Figure 8. Schematic diagram of the transverse section of deciduous oak. Diagram © Sara Rich, 2017.

facilitate quick outward expansion, after which cell growth slows at the onset of summer, diminishing further in autumn, and ceasing altogether in winter, thus indicating the terminus of the ring boundary (Figures 7, 8). These macro anatomical features, along with the presence of medullary rays, make it rather easy to identify oak in the field.

Furthermore, the large early-wood cells grown during the spring are vulnerable areas in the wood, where **tangential** breakage is most likely to occur. It is possible that for this reason, frames were often **converted** from young, fast-grown oaks: their lifespans included fewer springs, and therefore their wood has fewer weak spots when under pressure tangentially. On the other hand, planks converted from mature or slower-grown oaks posed no additional risk since the stress is distributed elsewhere in horizontally placed timbers. As a result, longitudinal timbers like planks, stringers, keels, and keelsons may be more likely to have the >80 **annual growth rings** required for tree-ring dating, while frames, stanchions, and other vertical elements often have only 30-60 rings, typically insufficient for **cross-dating** and thus provenancing through dendrochronology. In other words, timber of great size may not produce a great number of rings, and this seems particularly true of vertically placed oak timbers in Iberian vessels. However, these same vertically placed timbers are much more likely to retain **sapwood** and the **waney edge** than planks whose edges have normally been trimmed of the outermost rings; therefore, these timbers will be the more likely to provide a felling date, and thus a date of construction and location for the source wood, than planks alone. In some cases, samples retaining bark edge can even be dated to the season during which the parent tree was felled. If there is sapwood data on file for the region where the tree was felled (as is the case for Northern European oaks outside of Iberia), then the missing sapwood rings may be estimated within a few years of the felling date (Hughes et al. 1981; Sohar et al. 2012). Even if a sample retains no bark edge or sapwood and/or cannot be cross-dated due to insufficient ring count, there are numerous laboratory analyses that do not require a large number of **annual growth rings** for which the sample may prove productive (Figure 5; 3.3). In sum, it is always best to sample multiple different timber elements dispersed throughout the shipwreck assemblage.

While frames tend to be composed of **hardwoods** like oak, especially during the Early Modern period (for earlier periods see Steffy 2001; Guibal & Pomey, 2003; Crumlin-Pedersen & Olsen 2002; Rival 1991), planks and wales are often composed of soft **coniferous** woods, usually pine (*Pinus* L.; Figures 7, 9).

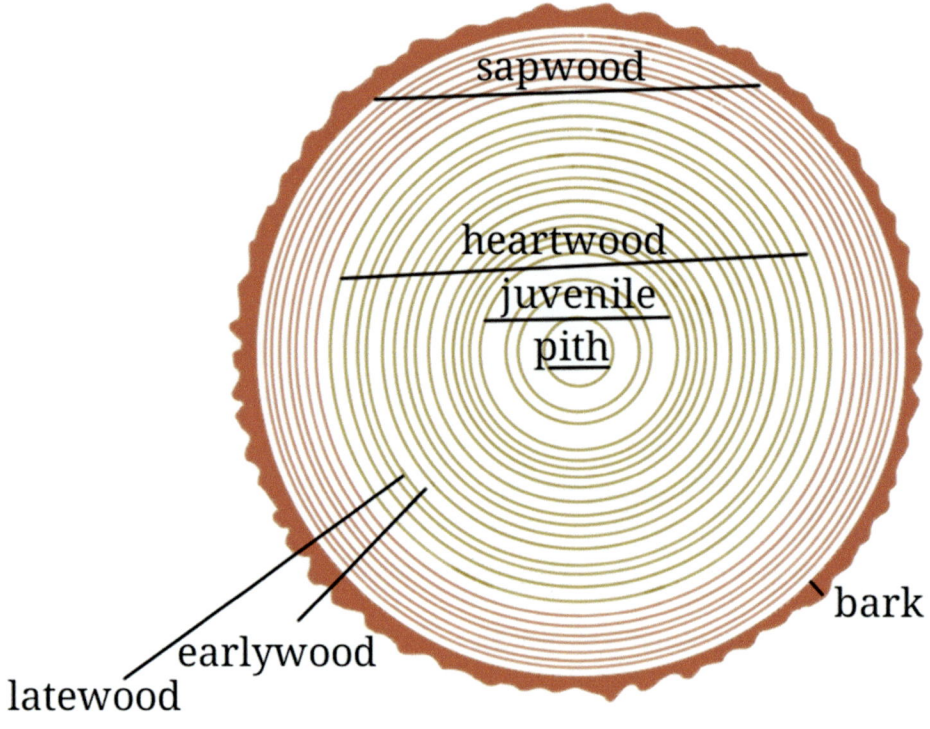

Figure 9. Schematic diagram of the transverse section of a coniferous wood. Diagram © Sara Rich, 2017.

Conifers contain high amounts of **resin** that make their wood more resistant to rot and fungal attacks, and **softwood** is easier to **convert** and conform to bespoke shapes, whether building in the shell-first or frame-first method (Steffy 2001; Guibal & Pomey 2003). Pine growth rates are highly variable, but like oak, they can be long-lived trees, and those from mountainous environments are highly suitable for dendrochronology (Domínguez-Delmás et al., in prep; Schweingruber 2012). Samples of pine ceiling planks of the wrecked frigate, *Santa María Magdalena*, have also shown potential for provenancing through organic chemical analyses (Trindade et al., in press).

For analyses like dendrochronology that require large numbers of tree rings, the best planks to sample are those that were converted **radially**. Radial conversion means that the tree was divided from the center, or **pith**, out toward the bark, as in the rays of the sun (Figure 10). This method was used commonly in shipbuilding of the Northern European Middle Ages when **converting** oak stems to hull planks for clinker construction; each plank was split with an axe along the medullary rays of the **transverse** section (Crone & Barber 1981; Crumlin-Pedersen & Olsen 2002). The result is not only a stronger length of wood more resistant to warping, but also an ideal surface for the measurement of **annual growth rings**, and by extension, growth anomalies that could implicate origin. The two short ends of the plank will feature the radius of the transverse section, revealing a ring sequence, ideally, from **pith** to **sapwood** (Figure 10). Radially converted timbers are also relatively easy to spot underwater, given the right conditions. If the largest face of the plank appears to be composed of straight lines extending the length of the timber (Figure 10), as opposed to seeing the grain of the wood (Figure 11), then it is probably radially converted.

In the Early Modern period, the advent of carvel construction in Northern Europe coincides with the tangential conversion of hull planking by sawing, which resulted in decreased amounts of wood waste

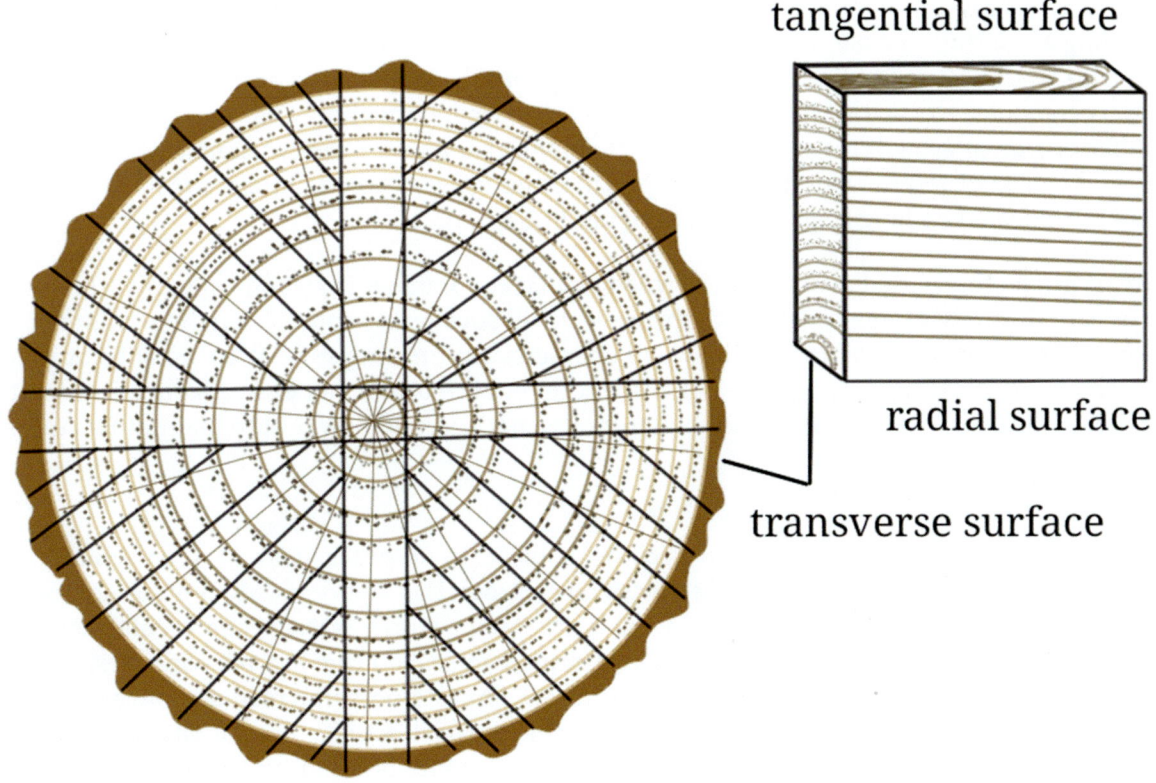

Figure 10. Schematic diagram of the radial conversion of deciduous oak. Diagram © Sara Rich, 2017.

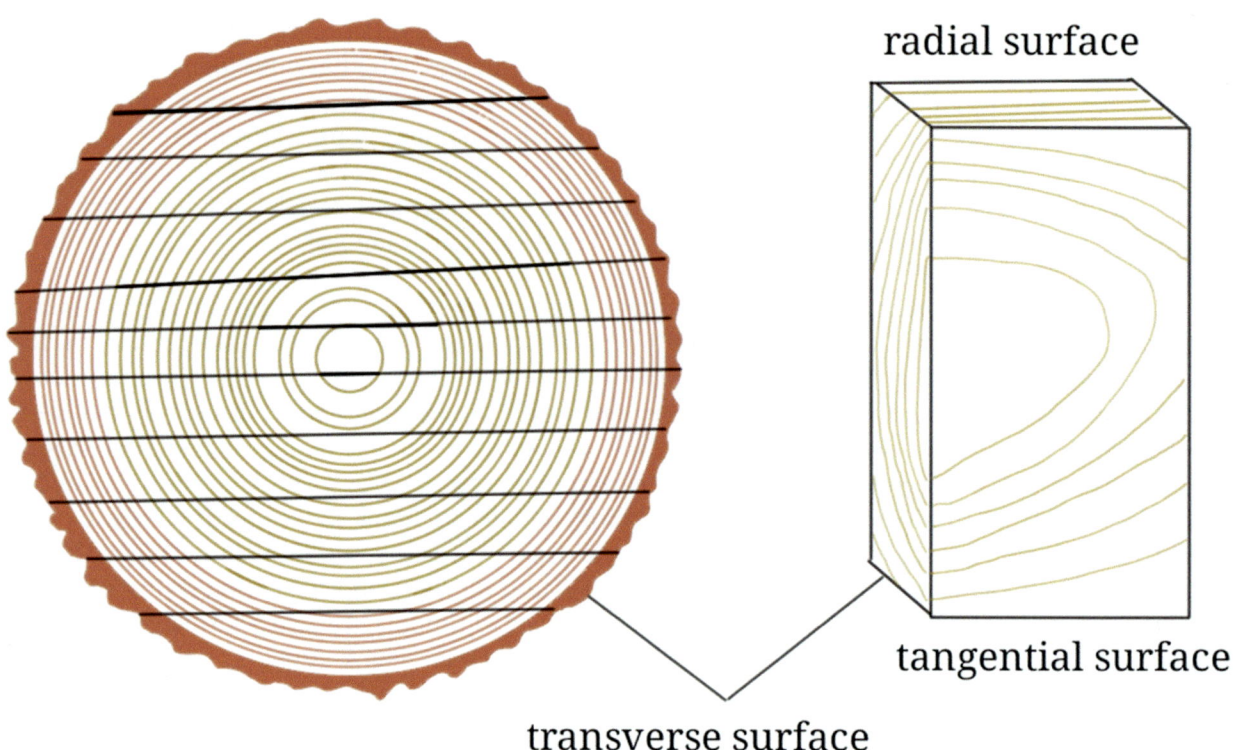

Figure 11. Schematic diagram of the tangential conversion of a coniferous wood. Diagram © Sara Rich, 2017.

(Figure 11). It has been hypothesized that these technological and industrial changes occurred in response to decreasing amounts of wood available to shipbuilders due to deforestation (Crespo Solana & Nayling 2016; Phillips 1986, 51, notes that ¼ of the total wood mass was lost during conversion, even with the saw). Because the line of the saw runs tangentially to the curve of the annual growth rings (or perpendicular to the rays), tangentially converted timbers will only rarely retain the requisite number of annual growth rings for dendrochronological analysis. Even so, samples of these timbers may still be submitted to laboratories engaged in other types of wood characterization studies that are not predicated on long ring sequences (Figure 5; 2.1, 3.3).

Conversion methods used in altering the wood from tree to timber is just one more consideration to factor in to the timber sampling strategy the project will develop. As noted throughout this document, the number of samples required by the wood characterization analyst must be weighed against the research questions being asked (Figure 4), the resources of time and money available to answer those questions, the overall condition of the shipwreck assemblage, and how best to maintain its integrity.

3.1.1. Assemblage and preservation

Like any archaeological site, a shipwreck is subject to a great deal of environmental and anthropogenic change. Tidal currents can wash away protective layers of sediment, or deforestation upstream can lead to thick soil dumps in the delta. Major storm systems can create scour marks on the seafloor, and trawlers can leave trails of disturbed seabed that stretch for miles. These and myriad other environmental factors may have direct impacts on shipwreck assemblages and how they are preserved *in situ*. Of course, invasive archaeological activity on the site will affect it as well (See Chapter 5). Therefore, non-invasive methods should be used first prior to sampling any timber. Mapping, sketching, taking GPS points, and taking advantage of imaging methods such as **photogrammetry**, will help ensure that any sample taken has a recorded provenance in relation

Figure 12. Diver photographs ship timbers *in situ* at the Yarmouth Roads shipwreck site (Isle of Wight, UK). These digital photographs contribute to the ongoing 3D model of the site. Photograph by Beñat Eguíluz Miranda, © Maritime Archaeology, Ltd., 2016.

to the assemblage and the surrounding seabed (Figure 12). Months and even years after a sampling campaign, questions of archaeological context are certain to arise. Was that plank section removed from the port or starboard side? That frame from the bow or stern? These are questions that should be answered easily through adequate recording.

An assessment of the geophysical environment and the condition of the shipwreck assemblage will also inform which timbers could provide samples of the greatest scientific value. Badly degraded timbers will likely be of little value outside genus or species identification. Of course, this is an important step toward understanding the ship, but used alone, it is unlikely to provide a reliable provenance (2.1.2). Instead, focusing efforts on timbers in good condition will furnish samples that can be used for multiple analyses (Figure 5). Even so, a timber may appear to be in very good condition, but when sawing, it becomes clear that the interior is more mollusk tunnel than wood. If a massive oak log has never been so easy to cut through, there is a good chance that it is not worth even that much effort. It is better to leave it in place and look elsewhere. The best chances for finding timbers with the least amount of erosional or **xylophagic** damage is under the seabed, which may require additional licensing (Figure 13; see Chapter 4; Björdal & Gregory 2011; Palma & Santhakumaran 2014).

Fundamentally, archaeologists should not take more samples than can realistically be processed. Responsibilities for post-excavation analyses, including documentation and storage, should be weighed realistically (3.2). Furthermore, taking a timber sample is an irreversible step toward the vessel's eventual disintegration. This too is a big responsibility, and archaeologists need to consider the long-term impacts of their decisions of where to sample and how many to take.

Generally speaking, a reasonable rule of thumb for the best results is to supply analysts with 20-50 samples per vessel, with each sample representing a different timber, and ideally, from a different area of the ship (laterally and longitudinally). From the analyst's perspective, more is always better; however, the economic law of diminishing returns also applies to samples, stating that eventually, more is not better (Orton 2000, 7; Domínguez-Delmás et al., in prep, b). Statistically, it is better to have fewer high-quality samples than dozens of low-quality. As a rough, conservative estimate, and in particular for ships built of Iberian timber, only 50% of samples taken will prove useful for dendrochronology, which shares some sample requirements with anatomical and molecular marker analyses (Figure 5; 3.3). As an example, a wrecked 16th century galleon in Ribadeo (Galicia, Spain) has seen two sampling campaigns, producing 29 and 19 samples respectively of mostly oak (with two of pine in the latter campaign; see Figure 13; for the results of the first campaign, see: Domínguez-Delmás 2013). Of these 48 samples, only 35 could be used for dendrochronology, and even then, the samples could not be **cross-dated** between themselves or with established chronologies. Therefore, they – and the ship – remain absolutely and relatively undated (M. Domínguez-Delmás, pers. comm.).

While we must always be mindful of the integrity of the site, if a shipwreck has recently been exposed and its wood is at risk of eminent deterioration (or anthropogenic destruction), it would be wise to concentrate efforts on taking a few extra samples from this site, as there may not be a chance to return to it in the same condition if at all. After the first dive or two on the site, archaeologists should have sufficient information to develop an underwater sampling strategy (Figure 6; see Orton 2000, 179-184; Nayling in Coles & Goodburn 1991).

3.1.2. Sampling underwater

In many cases, shipwreck sampling campaigns will be conducted underwater, in conditions that range from 20m of visibility to none, and from calm friendly waters to those with dangerous tidal currents. Every body of water has its own 'personality', and that can change wildly from day to day, or even within the same day. Clearly, the safety of the divers is more important than getting that last **cross-section**. Sawing large timbers underwater requires a great deal of physical exertion, and divers should be prepared to extend their usual air consumption rate by two or three times. There are also associated dangers of using saws, usually rusty ones, underwater, where lacerations can easily occur without the diver even being aware of them. In our experience, FatMax® saws from Stanley® with BladeArmor® coating have been worth the investment; they have an effective saw-tooth pattern that facilitates faster sawing (and thus less time, energy, and air spent), and the coating helps to prevent rust development on the blade (Figure 14). In salt-water environments, rust renders most saws worthless after a single dive. To reduce friction when sawing, wax or another kind of lubricant (e.g., WD-40®) may be helpful, but these pose issues of sample contamination for chemical and DNA analyses and are better avoided if there is any intention of submitting samples to laboratories running these kinds of tests (Figure 5; 3.3). In any case, lubricants used on the saw should be noted on the sample record (3.2). **Increment borers**, hollow drill-like tools used to remove **core samples**, cannot reasonably be used underwater. There is limited leverage whereby to screw the borer into the wood, and even if that is achieved, waterlogged samples come out mangled beyond recognition or use. Furthermore, damage to the wood by marine borers prevents the core sample's ability to reflect the tree's growth due to the replacement of **annual growth rings** with **teredo galleries**. Besides using a wood saw, the only other currently available tool is a chainsaw; however using a chainsaw underwater can only be done by hard-hat divers on **surface supply**, not by **SCUBA** divers.

Figure 13. Samples of framing elements from two different shipwrecks; all four sampled timbers were converted from fast-grown, short-lived oak trees. Left: excavated samples in good condition with preserved sapwood on elongated corners from the bow of the Yarmouth Roads shipwreck (Isle of Wight, UK). Right: exposed teredo-ridden samples with preserved sapwood (lighter in colour) from the wrecked sixteenth-century galleon at Ribadeo (Galicia, Spain). Photographs by Sara Rich, © Maritime Archaeology, Ltd., 2015.

Other practical concerns include recording and labeling. As mentioned above, timbers must be recorded *in situ* before being sampled (3.1; Figure 15). The timbers to potentially be sampled should be labeled with a unique number or code that is visible underwater to diver and camera and that is securely fixed to the timber. In deep or calm waters like the Mediterranean, stainless steel single-use injection needles may be sufficient to hold tags in place; in shallow waters or those with strong tidal currents like the English Channel, long copper nails hammered into thick plastic labels, or even cattle tags, work best (Figure 16).

Once the timber is labeled and recorded with its label *in situ*, it may be sampled. Ziplock bags (or other sterile container) to hold samples should be prepared with labels before the diver enters the water (Figure 15). Labels should be written using markers with permanent black or blue ink on both sides of the label. The text should identify the site and the parent timber at least (ex: Magdalena 046). Labels could

Figure 14. Diver removes a cross-section of pine hull planking from the wrecked eighteenth-century frigate *La Santa Maria Magdalena* (Galicia, Spain). The ends of the planking were not accessible, so samples were removed from the center. Photograph by Adolfo Miguel Martins, © Maritime Archaeology, Ltd., 2015.

also be prepared to conform to the appropriate units of the database code that will be used to organize data produced during excavation and analysis (ex: MAG01-046W-001S; 3.2.5). Because everything is more difficult underwater, even things like opening a ziplock bag, or finding the right label for the right sample, can be frustrating and time consuming. To make these otherwise simple matters easier, open the ziplock bags that will be used before entering the water; they will be buoyant at first but will then fill with water and become a negligible nuisance as opposed to a persistent one. As for managing the labels underwater, have them prepared beforehand on a binder ring or carabiner (or both connected together): place the labels in numerical order, punch a hole in the ordered stack, and string the labels onto the ring. Underwater, the correct label can be found easily and torn from the ring before placing it in the container with the sample, and sealing the container. At the surface, the container should also be labeled so that it matches the loose label inside with the sample. Both container and loose label should also be dated with the date the sample was taken and the dive number and/or initials of who took the sample. Samples with missing or confused labels may have to be discarded, so it is essential that labeling is taken seriously.

Besides being efficient, effective, and safe underwater, sampling divers should also find a balance between enthusiasm and realism in terms of the number of samples to be taken. Likewise, sampling unique ship features should also be approached with caution. In the example of a campaign on the *Bayonnaise* (a late eighteenth-century French corvette off the coast of northern Spain), on the next to last

> **EXAMPLE OF AN UNDERWATER SAMPLING PROCEDURE**
>
> 1. Label and record timbers *in situ* that may be suitable for sampling in accordance with sampling strategy and research questions.
> 2. Prepare sterile plastic containers by opening them before entering the water.
> 3. Prepare labels for samples to be removed that indicate the site and the parent timber before entering the water.
> 4. Identify the area of the timber that will provide the most possible data.
> 5. Remove the sample in the form of a cross-section (3-5cm thick) from the timber.
> 6. Place it in the prepared container along with the label, and secure the container.
> 7. Carefully bring the samples to the surface.
> 8. Fill out detailed dive log including samples taken and from which timbers at which areas of the shipwreck.
> 9. Label the sample container with the same information as the label.
> 10. Clean the sample with cool fresh or salt water.
> 11. Record the sample while keeping it moist, noting sources of possible contamination.
> 12. Store the sample in its container inside another larger container (plastic tote box) that is also filled with cool fresh or salt water.
> 13. Store containers with samples in a cool, dark place.
> 14. Deliver or hand off the container with samples to the wood analyst, along with copies of the sample record sheet.
> 15. Enter data from dive log and sample record sheet into spreadsheet or database.
> 16. Report activities to the necessary heritage agencies.
> 17. Patiently await the results of analyses!

Figure 15. Example of the step-by-step procedure for removing a wood sample from a shipwreck underwater.

day of the field season, two divers were using a dredge to excavate sand from an area of semi-exposed timbers. Unexpectedly, they exposed the keelson. A sample of the keelson would be nearly unmatched in terms of value for **dendroprovenance** studies. It is likely to have been formed of a long-lived tree, such as oak or pine, for which reference chronologies are likely to exist. However, when the divers returned to the area to record (photographs, measurements from fixed points, and drawings) before removing a sample, they realized that this very important feature could not be recorded sufficiently in the time they had left to work on the site. On the spot, they made the difficult decision to not destroy the integrity of the timber and instead backfilled it with sand. Making these kinds of judgment calls are difficult enough, but even more so when mental faculties are stunted by the effects of being underwater, even at shallower depths. This too is an unavoidable aspect of working in this unique environment and one that archaeologists should be prepared to face and factor into their diving and sampling strategies (Figure 6).

Divers should also try to collect samples that will be useful for the greatest variety of analyses (Figure 5; 3.3). For example if bark or the soft outer rings, **sapwood**, is visible, that is a good indicator that this timber would be worth sampling because it is useful for many different analyses, including dendrochronology. When possible, a close inspection of the **transverse** section of a timber will also help the diver decide whether or not the sample would be worthwhile. If the **annual growth rings** are visible, check to see how narrow they are. Timber adapted from slow-grown, long-lived trees is likely to provide more information relevant to **dendroprovenance** than trees that were only a few decades old

FIGURE 16. A SERIES OF SAMPLED HULL PLANKS *IN SITU* AT THE YARMOUTH ROADS SHIPWRECK (ISLE OF WIGHT, UK) DEMONSTRATING TANGENTIAL CONVERSION, WHICH PRESERVES ONLY A FEW ANNUAL GROWTH RINGS OF RELATIVELY SLOW-GROWN AND MODERATELY LONG-LIVED TREES. SAMPLES WERE REMOVED FROM THE ENDS OF THE EXPOSED PLANKS. PHOTOGRAPH BY MARTIN DAVIES, © MARTIN DAVIES AND MARITIME ARCHAEOLOGY, LTD., 2016.

when felled, as explained above (3.1). Again, it is essential to remember that great size is not necessarily an indicator of great age.

In any case, it will be beneficial prior to removing the sample to consider from where on the parent tree the timber originated. If the sample is removed from an area where branches formed on the tree, the presence of knots will make the sample more difficult cut through, while distorting the visible ring pattern (Figure 17). Whether the parent tree grew in a densely forested landscape or one that was carefully managed, samples should be removed from areas that correspond with lower on the stem, or if curved and likely **converted** from a limb, in the center away from branches and knots (Figure 17).

An unexpected difficulty that divers encounter while sampling is that taking the sample is too easy; that is to say that the timber selected to sample looks to be in pristine condition but has actually been badly degraded by **xylophagic** molluscs, such as teredo or piddock (Palma & Santhakumaran 2014). It is often impossible to tell before beginning to saw into the timber, but particularly with large oak timbers that should be highly laborious to sample, it becomes soon all too clear that the interior of the timber has been eaten away and is actually more **teredo gallery** than **xylem**. In many cases, it may be better to abandon taking this sample in lieu of one from a better preserved timber that poses fewer road blocks of contamination or accurate ring-width measurement in the lab (Figure 13; section 3.1.2).

Practically speaking, if the ends of the timber are accessible and in good condition (minimal teredo or other damage seen), a **cross-section**, 3-5cm thick, can be removed from the end with a single cut (Figure

CHAPTER 3 SAMPLING AND SUB-SAMPLING

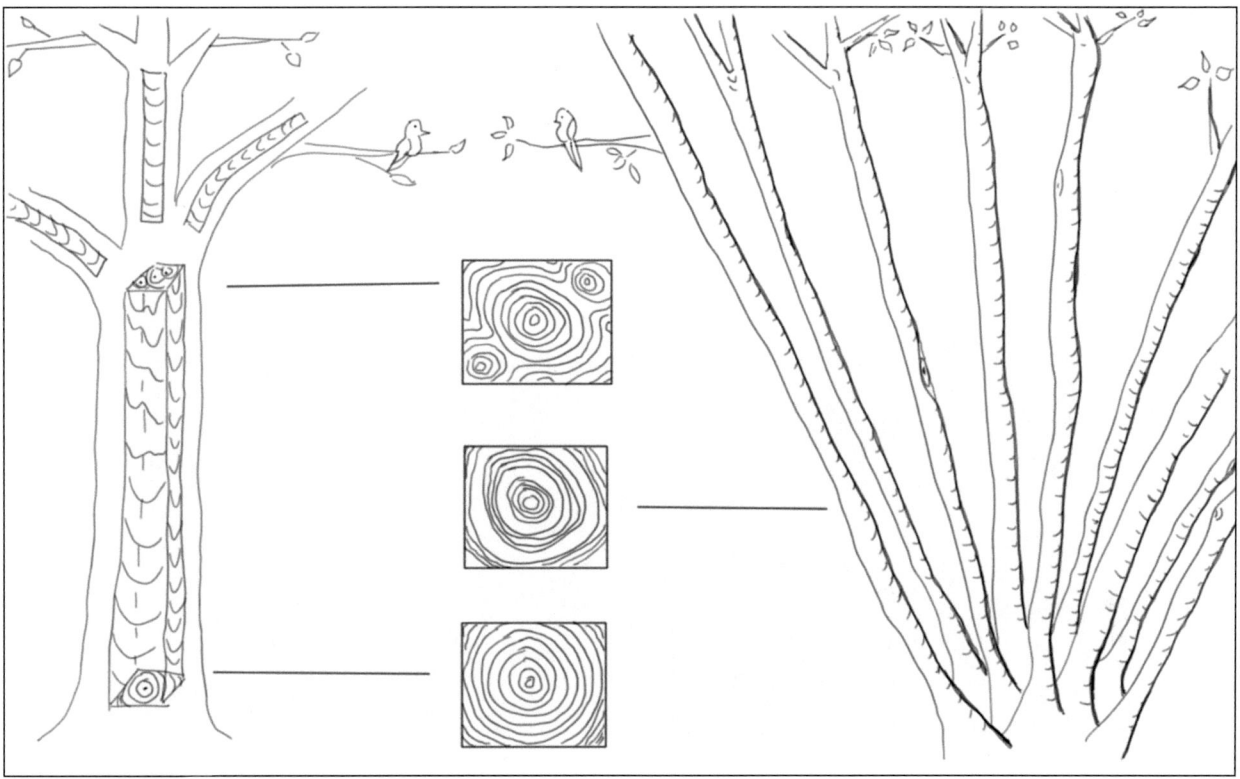

FIGURE 17. CROSS-SECTIONS REMOVED FROM DIFFERENT PARTS OF THE SAME TIMBER MAY SHOW DIFFERENT RECORDS OF THE PARENT TREE'S GROWTH. CROSS-SECTIONS FROM LIMBS OR FURTHER UP THE STEM WILL BE MORE LIKELY TO DISPLAY WARPED RING-WIDTH PATTERNS DUE TO BRANCHING AND KNOTS, WHILE THOSE TAKEN FROM AREAS CORRESPONDING WITH THE BASE OF THE STEM WILL BE MORE LIKELY TO DISPLAY A RING-WIDTH PATTERN THAT CORRESPONDS MORE ACCURATELY WITH THE WHOLE TREE'S GROWTH (LEFT). THOSE SAMPLING WILL DO WELL TO KEEP IN MIND WHERE A CERTAIN SHIP TIMBER WOULD HAVE ORIGINATED WITHIN THE PARENT TREE. RING-WIDTH PATTERNS MAY ALSO DEMONSTRATE THE ORIGINAL LANDSCAPE, SUCH AS FORESTED OR OPEN, AND WHETHER OR NOT THE PARENT TREE HAD BEEN MANAGED THROUGH COPPICING (RIGHT). DRAWING © SARA RICH, 2017.

16); otherwise, the sample can be removed from a better preserved or accessible area in the middle of the timber with two cuts (Figures 14, 18). However, the more cuts made, the more time is spent underwater and the more unstable the assemblage may become. Therefore, if the **transverse** section is not visible or not accessible (i.e., the ends are overlain by other wreckage or joined to other timbers, they are buried beneath a great deal of sediment, or the ends are badly degraded), a **wedge sample** may be removed before committing to a cross-section in the middle of the timber (Nayling in Coles & Goodburn 1991). In taking a wedge sample, the saw is positioned centrally along the timber but at an acute angle. After cutting down a few centimeters, the saw is removed and then placed further down the timber and at an opposite angle so that the cuts will join a few centimeters into the timber, and a wedge-shaped piece of wood can be removed (Figure 19). This acts as a kind of pre-sample, allowing the wood specialist to determine if this timber would be worth spending a whole dive, or even two, to cut a cross-section from.

Because samples are representative of both the ship and the forest where they originated, it is also important to collect a variety of wood and timber types for **dendroprovenance**: not just planks, but also frames, beams, stanchions, etc., and not just oak, but also pine, chestnut, or that mysterious reddish-colored timber that might be representative of a repair in some exotic location where oak and pine were unavailable. Clearly, information from repairs will not disclose the ship's construction site, but it is an important factor in understanding the vessel's working life. Again, the types of samples to target depend entirely on the research questions being asked (Figure 4).

Figure 18. Hull planking samples from two different shipwrecks; each sample was converted from a slow-grown, long-lived tree. Top: tangentially converted pine planking with preserved sapwood (on left) from the wrecked eighteenth-century frigate *La Santa Maria Magdalena* (Galicia, Spain). Bottom: radially converted oak planking with preserved sapwood (on right) from the Yarmouth Roads shipwreck (Isle of Wight, UK).
Photographs by Sara Rich, © Maritime Archaeology, Ltd., 2016.

Figure 19. Wedge sample removed from a slow-grown oak timber composing the wrecked eighteenth-century frigate *La Santa Maria Magdalena* (Galicia, Spain). Photographs by Sara Rich, © Maritime Archaeology, Ltd., 2015.

There are those unfortunate cases when the ideal timber is spotted, but it is impossible to sample. This may be due to the presence of iron fittings that cannot be sawn through, or because the saw cannot fit between the desired timber and the one next to it. In many other cases, the timber section is sawn halfway through only to encounter a nail. Sometimes nails can be broken through with a hammer and chisel, and other times, the half-sawn sample must be abandoned. On the other hand, especially with **softwood** or timbers from older shipwrecks, the saw may be abandoned altogether. During fieldwork on site in 2015, author Rich sampled the pine hull planking from a Late Classical Greek shipwreck off the coast of Cyprus (see Demesticha 2011). The desired plank (**radially** converted with estimated >80 rings) was situated on the edge of the trench, so the saw was easily used to cut back from the edge toward the opposite side of the trench and the rest of the hull. However, there reached a point when to go further back with the saw would mean damaging the plank next to the one being sampled. In this case, the saw was set aside and a putty knife put to work in its stead. The wood was soft enough that the putty knife cut through without even needing to be hammered. The sample was removed with a trowel rather like lifting a large piece of cake from a plate. It was then wrapped in burlap and secured with ropes in a purpose-prepared crate, and gently toted the 45m back up to the surface.

In another scenario, due to the limitations of time and challenging conditions underwater, only three samples from the Yarmouth Roads shipwreck (a supposed sixteenth-century carrack) were able to be removed (Rich et al., in press; Rich & Satchell 2016; Rich et al. 2015). These **cross-sections** contained **pith** and **sapwood**, and they were very well preserved within the clay seabed (Figure 13). This all bodes well for dendrochronology, but for reasons stated above regarding construction with oak frames (3.1), the ring counts were insufficient for **cross-dating**. Furthermore, because the trees were young (ranging from 24-45 years old), their **annual growth rings** represent 'juvenile growth': that is, like human adolescents, trees also experience growth spurts and stunts that may be irrespective of the factors – such as nutrition, hydration, health, and environmental conditions – that dictate to a large degree the growth patterns of adult trees (Figures 8 and 9). In other words, erratic juvenile rings are often unusable for dendrochronology as well as for anatomical and molecular marker analyses that also depend on the indicators of relationships between growth and environment. So again, a greater number of samples from a variety of ship timbers helps to maximize the potential for several **dendroprovenance** techniques to be applied to a single shipwreck assemblage (Figure 5; 3.3).

3.1.3. Sampling on land

Shipwrecks are not necessarily found underwater, and historical ships are not necessarily wrecked. In many cases, nautical archaeologists do not even have to get wet to do their job, although they may get rather muddy. Two examples are provided here: the first is the Newport Ship, a vessel that had been abandoned in mid-repair on the banks of the River Usk in Wales and eventually silted over, and which has been dated to the mid-late 15th century through dendrochronology and numismatics (Nayling & Susperregi 2014); the other, the Belinho shipwreck, is a disarticulated vessel of suspected 16th-century date, whose timbers have recently washed ashore in Portugal after a series of storms in the Atlantic. While the general guidelines of timber selection for dendroprovenance are the same underwater and on land, recovering and sampling ship timbers in rescue- or development-led projects comes with a few of its own caveats leading to possibilities for different recording and sampling strategies (Domínguez-Delmás et al., in prep, b).

One of the main differences between sampling campaigns on land and those underwater is time. With the possibility of longer working days spent in the direct company of the timbers themselves instead of dealing with the logistics of how to get to them, recording and sampling processes can be expedited and made much more thorough, comparatively speaking. The other major difference is the tools at one's disposal: namely **increment borers**, but also non-invasive techniques like high-res scale photography and CT scanning (Bill et al. 2012).

The Newport Ship was excavated from the mud timber by timber, with each one being recorded and conserved before reintroduced to the reconstructed vessel. Each of the 2000 timbers was cleaned and placed in a shallow tank to keep it waterlogged, and then each was recorded using the FARO® FaroArm along with 3D software from Rhinoceros (Jones 2013; see also Vermeersch & Haneca 2015 and Vermeersch et al. 2015). Painstaking recording of individual timbers allowed the vessel to be digitally reconstructed while at the same time capturing the patterns of cut marks, fastening, and details of **conversion** necessary to track what kinds of forests these timbers came from. Once the structural timbers were recorded, some were selected to sample for dendrochronological dating and provenance. The samples were selected based on the number of rings and the presence of **sapwood** or even **waney edge**, as was present on the keel. The majority of the samples were taken from the outer perimeter of vessel, which revealed wood from slower grown trees than those found in the inner sections. Fifty planks or strakes (13%) from port and starboard sides and 39 framing timbers (15%) from around the outer perimeter of the ship were sampled. These planks produced the samples that came to compose the vessel's object chronology through averaged ring-width measurements, which were then used to **cross-date** the ship timbers against regional chronologies (2.1.1). For some timbers, a wedge sample of sapwood and outermost **heartwood** rings was taken first, followed by a **core sample** to add the inner heartwood rings to the sequence (cf. Figure 19). Each sample was converged via the overlapping rings to represent the full timber and the tree from which it was derived (Nayling & Susperregi 2014).

Following the example of the Newport Ship project, sampling timbers washed ashore from the Belinho shipwreck combined an ambitious agenda of digital recording techniques and sampling for six different **dendroprovenance** methods (Castro et al., 2015; Martins et al., in press). Given the availability of space on land to undertake such a study, timber characterization was a primary aim in order to develop a relationship between the construction of the ship and the source forests that provided its timbers.

Some seventy timbers were recorded using digital photography, FaroArm or laser scanning, and those that met the criteria for dendrochronology (>50 rings) were sampled with the other dendroprovenance analyses in mind as well. Planks were sampled by removing a section, and frames were sampled using an **increment borer**. Work accomplished on the Belinho shipwreck is an excellent example of how ship timbers – individually and collectively – can contribute to an understanding of how timbers were converted from parent trees, what those parent trees looked like, and the kinds of environments in which they grew at the time of felling (Martins et al., in press).

On land, using an increment borer on the timbers is preferable to cutting a **cross-section**, particularly in cases such as the above where each timber was to be conserved for restoration (in full or part) of the ship (Domínguez-Delmás et al., in prep, b). Although its use underwater should not be attempted (see 3.1.2), an increment borer removes only a thin (ca. 4.3-5.15mm) cylindrical section of wood, so the damage to sampled timbers can be better minimized on land. An isotopic borer (12mm) can also be used which produces a sample thick enough that it can be subsampled for other analyses (e.g., Rich et al. 2012).

3.2. Post-excavation processing

As with the removal of any cultural object from an archaeological site, taking timber samples from a shipwreck means dealing with artefacts. Although construction timbers have historically been considered examples of 'non-artefactual wood', this view can no longer be sustained given the degree of deliberation behind each ship timber that makes its manufacturing process similar to that of any other carved or hewn wooden artefact (Crone & Barber 1981). Samples thereof should also be treated with care as waterlogged wood makes for an extremely fragile artefact. If these samples are broken, glue will do nothing to resolve the problem. Storage facilities should be fully equipped to retain the wood while it awaits its destination. And of course, in the meantime, *ex situ* as much as *in situ*, these artefacts must be fully cleaned and recorded before being passed on to wood science laboratories, where, depending on the analysis to be undertaken, the samples may ultimately be destroyed (Figure 5). Fortunately, there are many options available today for recording, and the storage needs of waterlogged wood for short periods of times can be adapted to numerous field situations (Figure 15; see also Historic England 2015c [2010a]; Bowens 2009).

3.2.1. Cleaning

Before detailed recording can begin, the sample should be thoroughly cleaned. It may seem that wood coming from underwater would already be clean, but this is rarely the case. As mentioned above, wood is best preserved beneath sediment, so remaining clay and mud will be brought to the surface along with the sample. Gently rubbing the soiled surface while softly rinsing with water will usually remove even clayey sediment patches. Often, sediments are most forcefully lodged within the cavities created by wood-boring organisms. Gently spraying with fresh or salt water will flush out the soil; however, those cavities may be hosting biogenic fillers as well as geogenic ones.

Wood-boring molluscs like piddock and teredo will frequently still be in the wood when it is surfaced. It is important to dispose of these animals while cleaning and before storage because if they are left inside, they will die, resulting in an unbearable odour that also attracts sea scavengers such as gulls. Besides flushing them out of their calcareous galleries with water, forceps or pincers may be helpful to reach into the bore-hole and pluck them out (Figure 13). Quickly removing the sealife from the sample will also help prevent biological contamination and further damage to the wood (see: 3.3).

After it is clean, and regardless of methods chosen for documenting the sample *ex-situ*, it should remain moist. This can be challenging when working in hot, dry climates where water can evaporate from wood in seconds. Keeping the sample misted or splashed with fresh or salt water will keep it hydrated and preserved during documentation processes. If it is not kept wet, the wood will experience shrinkage and distortion, which would be detrimental to analyses relying on accurate measurements of **annual growth rings** or sub-annual growth patterns (Figure 5; 3.3; Hamilton 1996; Historic England 2015c [2010a]).

3.2.2. Visual recording

The first option for recording a timber sample visually is by drawing it. Although a pencil and paper may seem an archaic practice compared to the wide array of contemporary digital techniques available, this method has the advantage of enabling the archaeologist to take the time to examine the details from multiple angles. Drawing involves close observation that can facilitate awareness of such features as tool marks, unusual planes, or joints, which could go unnoticed during hasty photographic recording. In many cases, the sample will not need to be drawn archaeologically, but a rough sketch to illustrate **conversion** method, notable features, and the **transverse** section (with growth rings and rays), will be a helpful and expedient way to 'get to know' the object and its potentials for **dendroprovenance** (Figure 20). Features noted through drawing or sketching may in turn provide invaluable information about the ship's construction and the processes used to **convert** the parent tree into the present ship's timber.

The ways in which to create digital visual records of artefacts are constantly expanding, while the options for doing so are becoming more cost-effective and more user friendly (Niven & Pierce-McManamon 2011). With a digital camera, which nearly everyone has these days, and certainly all archaeological projects, samples can be photographed with a scale to capture each side, the growth rate of the original tree (**transverse** section), and any other features that exhibit information about the timber or tree from which it came, and which it now represents. Because the samples will be waterlogged, glare can pose a problem, so ideally, samples can be superficially dried with a paper towel and photographed in **raking light** instead of full sunlight (see Figure 7). At least the first photograph of the sample should be

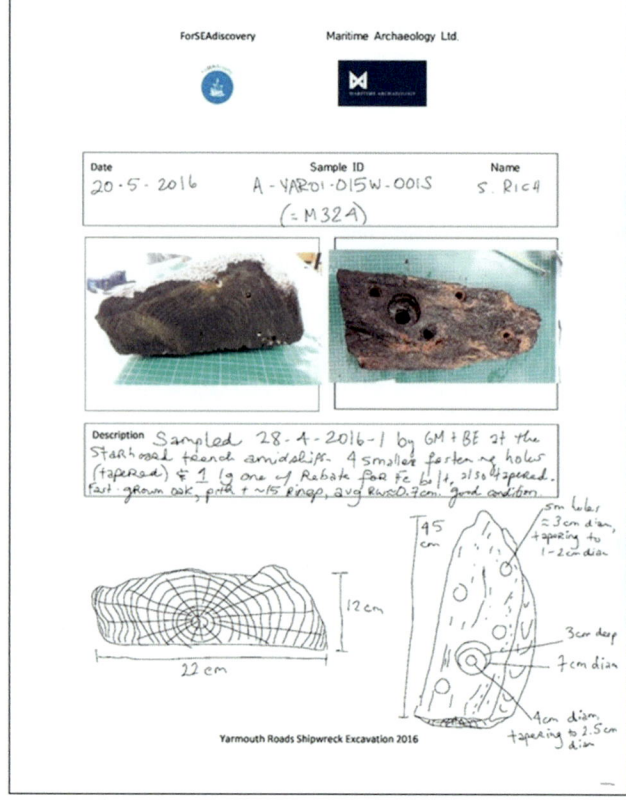
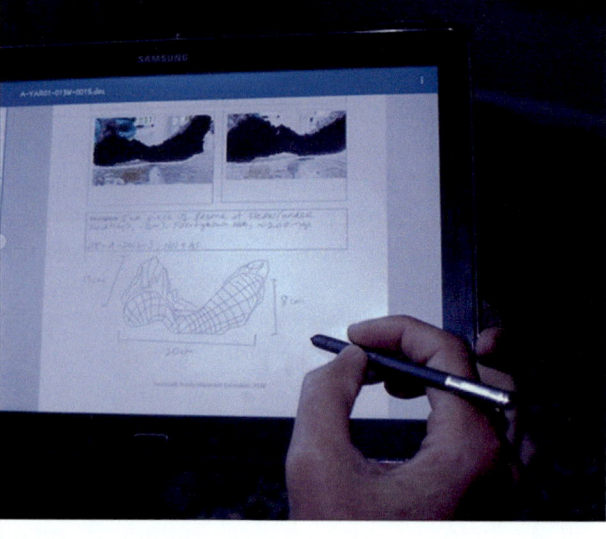

Figure 20. Timber sample record sheet produced on a Samsung Galaxy Note Pro 12.2 tablet.

taken with the label in the frame so that it is easier to identify which series of photographs are of which sample. This is especially important when processing multiple samples at a time.

Tablets provide a user-friendly way to consolidate record-keeping and minimize paper archives. One way to take advantage of this cost-effective and expedient technology is to create a digital template for a pro forma record sheet. A sheet can be filled out for each sample that includes a sketch, measurements, scale photographs, and text-based descriptions all together in the same document (Figure 20). Scale photographs can be directly integrated into the record sheet, which also minimizes the number of files to be stored and later archived (4.4). Digital record sheets are also easier to amend if a photograph needs to be re-shot or a text-based description requires more editing (3.2.3). If needed, the record sheets can be printed and filed, as record sheets have been produced and maintained by archaeologists for decades. Another advantage of the digital record sheet is its flexibility. Paper pro forma record sheets tend to be formulaic and do not easily allow for variations on the standard (Lucas 2001, 2012; Yarrow 2010). However, digital record sheets can be altered spontaneously to allow for an extra photograph or more room for a drawing or text, depending on the characteristics of the sample being recorded and the impressions of the one doing the recording.

For particularly unique samples that feature tool marks or an unusual **conversion** or joining method, archaeologists may wish to take visual recording to the next level. Two frequently used options, both of which can be conducted in the field, are photogrammetry and RTI (reflectance transformation imaging). Photogrammetry can be used to create **photomosaics** or 3D images, while RTI is a 2.5D imaging technique used to record subtle surface variations, such as tool marks, inscriptions, or makers' marks.

Photogrammetry involves taking a multitude of overlapping photos of the same object from as many angles as possible (Barnes 2011). To make a 3D image, the photographs are processed with specialized software (e.g., Agisoft) that transforms the pixel-based digital images into point clouds. If dense enough, the point cloud can produce a 3D image of the object. This .obj file can be uploaded to an online host, such as Sketchfab, or sent to a 3D printer. Photogrammetry is also increasingly being used underwater to record objects *in-situ* and even to document phases of shipwreck excavations (e.g., Demesticha et al. 2014). Other commonly used 3D timber recording methods include 3D laser scanning and FaroArm Contact 3D Digitiser (Jones 2013; Vermeersch and Haneca 2015; Vermeersch et al. 2015).

RTI requires slightly more equipment but is still possible to conduct in most field situations (Piquette & Crowther 2011). The high-res digital camera is mounted on a tripod in a dark room with a reflective object, such as a billiard ball, between the camera and the artefact being recorded. The camera and billiard ball remain stationary, while the flash goes off at various distances and angles from the artefact. The photographic files are then processed by computer software (RTI processing and viewing freeware is available from http://culturalheritageimaging.org) that overlaps the images into a single .rti file. The viewer can then change the lighting on the object to literally highlight the surface that reveals the most information. Besides its many archaeological and historical applications, this technique is also used by the FBI to capture notes written on pieces of paper that were torn away: the message imprinted on the sheet below is invisible to the naked eye, but RTI can make these faint marks legible again.

3.2.3. Text-based description

Text-based descriptions are also needed for each sample in order to record qualitative and quantitative information about the object. Height, width, thickness, and if possible, weight, should be documented because this information adds to existing databases on timber **scantlings** (see 1.3). Written descriptions of the sample's unusual features will complement the visual records and add substance to the project archive. The condition of the wood should also be described, noting the level of damage (either on a numerical scale or in descriptive terms), and its cause so that there is a record of accountability.

Of utmost importance, and something that cannot easily be relayed visually, is the archaeological context from where the sample originated. While the sample's context was recorded *in situ* before its removal, that information will be important to have on hand in numerous places. Furthermore, the context can also be important for the laboratory analyst who should be given copies of all descriptive forms along with the samples. Taking note of sediment type, depth, original versus inflicted damage, original size, and other factors will help clear up any discrepancies further down the road.

3.2.4. Storage

In most cases, the location of the fieldwork and the location of the lab(s) conducting analyses will not be the same. A plan for storing samples during this period between surfacing, recording, and wood science should already be in place before the field season begins (Figure 15).

In general, waterlogged wood should be kept wet, cool, and out of direct sunlight. Ideally then, temporary storage in a refrigerator would be a clever solution, especially in warm climates. However, this is not always possible, so other solutions could include keeping well-cleaned samples in large plastic containers filled with cool fresh or seawater (Figure 21). These containers can be kept in a garage, below decks, or any other place where they are as cool as possible and out of direct sunlight. Retaining water may need to be replaced every few days depending on ambient temperature so that the storage environment creates the fewest possibilities for rot or other biogenic damage to occur. As detailed below, biogenic contamination of samples can impede the results of several different **dendroprovenance** methods (Figure 5; 3.3).

Ideally, analysts will be prepared to receive samples within only a few days of their removal from the site. Whether storing or sending, each sample should be kept wet inside its own labeled container (Figure 21). If packing samples to mail or deliver to a laboratory for analysis, water and air surrounding the sample should be minimized before wrapping the ziplocked and labeled sample loosely in bubble wrap, foam, or other cushioning material (Figure 21). Samples should be kept like this for as short a time as possible, and still handled with great care.

3.2.5. Database management

Developing an effective database for recording archaeological fieldwork is an important part of every archaeological research project. When the project involves diving, *in-situ* recording, and sampling, the amount of records can quickly pile up. Databases not only help manage these records, but they can lay the essential groundwork for GIS- or web-based dissemination strategies (5.3). However, the database and the data itself must be structured correctly to be effective tools for researchers both inside and outside the project (Niven & Pierce-McManamon 2011). Data may be entered first into a spreadsheet, and then transferred into the database when the basic structure is more or less finalized, or a database can be used for data entry from the outset for its filter and search functions and to improve data compliance.

Data is organized by codes that indicate the type of data being referenced. This is usually a string of numbers and letters (units) that are organized from most broad to most specific, and which reference other elements in the database. For example, let's say we want the database to record the characteristics of a timber sample from the shipwrecked galleon at Ribadeo, Spain. The first unit within the code for this timber sample might start with the site code. This is an arbitrary configuration of numbers and letters, but the configuration must remain consistent, and it helps if it is obvious. For this site, we

CHAPTER 3 SAMPLING AND SUB-SAMPLING

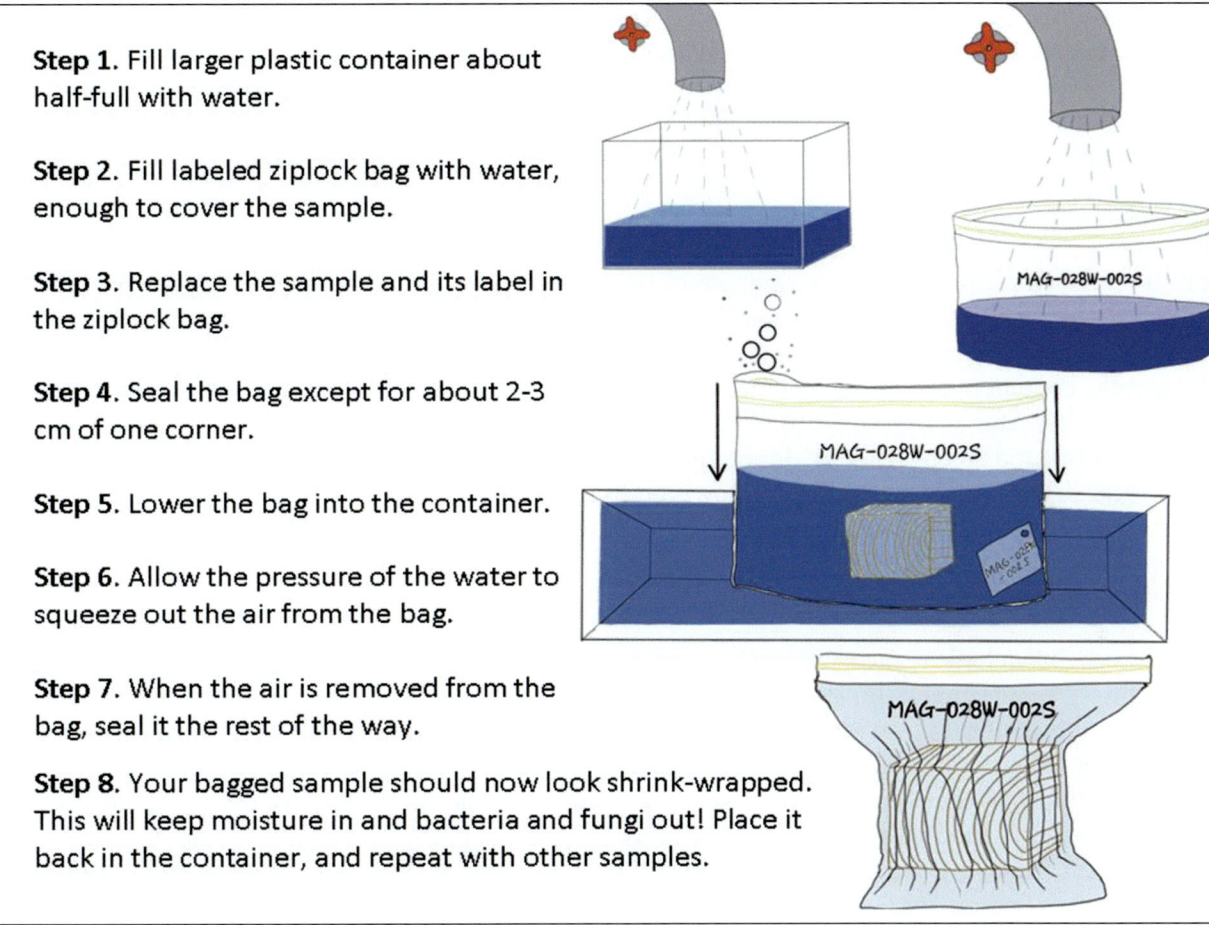

FIGURE 21. METHOD FOR STORING SAMPLES THAT PROTECTS AND KEEPS THE WOOD WET BUT REDUCES EXPOSURE TO AEROBIC BACTERIAL AND FUNGAL AGENTS. DRAWINGS © SARA RICH, 2017.

choose RIB01 – the first three letters of the location or name of the vessel when it sank, and a numerical code indicating order. The numerical order will become important if more than one vessel is discovered at the same site, as frequently occurs.

The second unit would reference the artefact within the site; in this case, the artefact would be the timber. So for example, the first timber labeled and recorded *in situ* might be labeled 001W, with the 'W' indicating the material type: wood. The fifteenth timber would be 015W, and so forth. However, other artefacts may be recorded and other types of samples removed from the site. The qualitative letter marker should always be placed at the end of the unit so that each numerical code is unique (i.e., there would never be wood, metal and ceramic artefacts with the same numerical code (W001, M001, C001); instead, each number is unique, and the letter simply serves to qualify the material. In this way, should the qualifier ever need to change, this can easily be done without disrupting the numerical order and introducing possible errors into the database. Now we have a string of RIB01-001W.

The third unit references the sample taken from this artefact. In our example, let us presume that there were three samples removed from the same timber. These could be identified as 01S, 02S, and 03S, where 'S' is for sample. This gives us a string of RIB01-001W-01S and so on.

Finally, as described below, if and when these samples are divided further, they can be assigned 01SS, where 'SS' is for sub-sample. This gives us a final string of RIB01-001W-01S-01SS, continuing numerically indefinitely. Naturally, this system can be adapted to the needs and aims of the project, as long as the ID codes are unique, representative, and searchable. Whatever coding system is used by a project, any given wood sample needs sufficient documentation to ensure that it is linked to the timber from which it was taken and preferably the location of that timber. Coding should also provide linkage to the relevant range of associated contextual records (dive logs, record sheets, etc.).

3.3. Sub-sampling

Ideally, each sample removed from a shipwreck will be sent to several different laboratories for different purposes. This is called sub-sampling. Each analysis listed above and below has different criteria to achieve the most reliable, accurate results: the size of the sample, from where in the tree it was **converted**, age of the sample, condition, etc. The following section describes ideal samples for each analysis as well as the minimum criteria for analysts (Figure 5). This information was provided by scientific analysts at European research institutions engaged in **dendroprovenance**, specifically of timber samples from Iberian shipwrecks of the 16th – 18th centuries. However, like much of the practical information presented here, these general criteria may also be applied to other archaeological contexts.

3.3.1. Dendrochronology

For dendrochronological measurements, contamination is not such a threat to accurate results. The primary requirements for a dendrochronology sample have to do with the orientation and the number and type of rings. An ideal sample should include >80 **annual growth rings** with **sapwood** and **waney edge** (Figures 8, 9). Samples that represent slow-grown, long-lived trees will provide the most amount of information (Figure 18). Complete **cross-sections** are ideal because even if the timber has been damaged by wood-boring organisms (especially gribble, piddock, and shipworm) or is otherwise damaged, accurate ring sequences can often still be constructed, albeit with greater difficulty (Figure 13; Domínguez-Delmás 2013). Waterlogged samples should be kept wet, as drying will lead to distortion in the rings (Figure 21). The **pith** can provide the first growth year of the tree, while the bark provides the last; even if the bark or bark edge is not retained though, the felling date of the tree can sometimes be estimated with sufficient sapwood rings. Clearly, in an underwater context, this ideal is not often met, so any **transverse** section with >50 is worth submitting for analysis. While coring along the radius of the stem is common on land, **increment borers** are not advisable for use underwater (see 3.1.2); instead whole cross-sections must be taken, such as the end sections of planks (see above, 3.1; Figure 16). However, because the analysis is not destructive to the sample, it can be reused for another analyses, such as anatomical and structural studies (Figure 5; see Domínguez-Delmás et al., in prep, b; Brewer & Jansma 2016; Historic England 2015a [1998]).

3.3.2. Dendroarchaeology

Typically, samples for dendroarchaeology are the same as they would be for species identification, so no great size or particular part of the tree is necessarily needed. Oftentimes, species identification is undertaken at the time of tree-ring analysis; however, there may be instances when a timber is unsuitable for dendrochronology, but having the wood type identified would contribute to the research questions (Figure 4). In these cases, an entire **cross-section** does not need to be removed from the timber in question. The sample should represent at least a few fully visible **annual growth rings**, and should also include **tangential** and **radial** sections, so a cohesive bit of wood 2-3cm^3 is typically sufficient. These samples could easily be taken from remnants of other analyses, such as dendrochronology, wood anatomy, DNA, or radiocarbon. In the vast majority of cases, species identification will be performed prior to any of the analyses discussed here, but it never hurts to seek multiple opinions, especially with such a low-cost method that offers a quick turnaround time.

However, a full cross-section could be provided to the analyst if a more holistic approach to dendroarchaeology is preferred: i.e., tree-ring studies without the **cross-dating**. In this case, the analyst would be looking for ring counts, average ring widths, presence of **sapwood** or **waney edge**, and **conversion** method.

3.3.1. DNA

Submitting wood samples for DNA analysis is different from collecting DNA for forensic evidence or for the human genome project, although contamination poses setbacks for both. Although samples of cambium or sapwood have traditionally been sought, recent methods of **PCR** amplification demonstrated no preference for a single type of wood (Gómez-Zeledón et al. 2017). Therefore, the wood sample may come from any part of the **converted** tree (Figure 17); however, it must be large enough that contaminated areas can be removed and still leave something over for the analysis, which requires at least enough wood to fill three 2mL reaction tubes. For dry wood, 400mg is recommended, but waterlogged wood samples should be considerably larger because in underwater contexts, wood is likely to be contaminated with mollusk shells from wood-boring organisms and a whole host of sea life (Figure 13). Regardless, anyone handling the sample should use sterile Latex gloves and avoid further contamination through bodily fluids (sweat, oil, blood, saliva, etc.). Storage of wet or waterlogged samples is problematic, as they cannot be held in paper (the usual recommendation), and sealed plastic containers can become breeding grounds for bacteria and fungi. If possible, samples are best kept refrigerated in an open container in fresh, clean water before handing over to the laboratory in a sealed ziplock bag (Figure 21).

3.3.4. Geochemistry

At the time of writing, geochemical methods require samples suitable for measurement with a **mass spectrometer**, and individual samples do not have to be more than a gram or two. However, when delivering a sample for these purposes, contamination factors into the minimum size needed, as does the need to run multiple destructive analyses on the same sample to ensure measurement and instrument consistency. Therefore, ideal samples will be at least 5cm^3 (or 50gr of a dry sample), so that contaminated areas, such as teredo galleries lined with calcite, can be removed and that sample divided up still further to run repeat measurements. The sample may be from any woody part of tree: **sapwood**, **heartwood**, branch, bark, or even twigs (Figures 8, 9, 17). It should be stored dry or refrigerated in clean water and a sterile plastic container (Figure 21). The turnaround time can take weeks or even months.

3.3.5. Anatomical and structural markers

Microscopic analysis of a wood sample for distinct anatomical markers is not destructive, and turnaround time can be quite fast, taking only a few days. The sample should include at least 40 growth rings, preferably from the stem of the source tree (Figure 17). This sample can be reused for and from dendrochronological investigations, and if no further contamination is introduced, it could be reused for structural and geochemical analyses or radiocarbon dating (Figure 5). The greater the sample size and number, the more representative the investigations can be of the entire tree.

While **FTIR** spectroscopy is non-destructive, **Py-GC/MS** is a destructive analysis (see: 2.1.5). In some cases however, samples can be reused from dendrochronology or wood anatomy, specifically if no chalk or wax (or other substance) has been applied to the surface of the material to enhance the appearance of ring boundaries.

Preferably, two samples per timber should be provided (again for instrument and measurement accuracy), and these should have minimal damage (scars, infestations, breakage, etc.). Ideally, the sample should be a core or **transverse** section that retains the **pith** and bark, or at least **sapwood** (Figures 8, 9). The turnaround time is similar to other spectrometer-dependent analyses, with roughly four weeks needed.

3.3.6. Radiocarbon (^{14}C)

There are no known applications of the ^{14}C **isotope** of carbon for provenance (unlike the stable isotope ^{13}C; see 2.1.4); however, it is included here briefly because it is one of the most common analyses undertaken on archaeological wood. Furthermore, because the archaeologist will likely sub-sample the initial shipwreck sample, it may be helpful to know what is needed to sub-sample for radiocarbon dating. Timber samples needed for ^{14}C analysis can be of only a few grams, but the samples should be representative of the felling date of the tree. For this reason, samples should be taken from the outermost rings (Figures 8, 9). This is because timbers cut from long-lived, slow-grown trees will often include hundreds of rings, each of which would provide a different date: i.e., a sample from the **pith** of such a tree would produce a date centuries older than the construction of the ship. Therefore one should be careful to sample wood from a single ring for a single date or the least number of rings possible (a bulk sample of ten rings is often used). In ideal circumstances, the radiocarbon sample of a single ring or group of rings would have a known age relationship with the felling date of the tree (using dendrochronology). Multiple samples from several ring locations with known ring-count intervals can be used to facilitate **^{14}C wiggle-match** dating which, combined with the use of Bayesian statistics, can model more precise dates than using only a single radiocarbon sample (e.g., Manning et al. 2014; Lorentzen et al. 2014). Wood taken for radiocarbon testing should be handled with latex gloves to avoid contamination, and samples should be kept separate in sterile plastic bags or boxes (Figure 21).

Chapter 4
Legal Considerations

Today, heritage is political. As a result, legal considerations for archaeological work underwater differ greatly depending on federal (or in some cases regional, state, provincial, or civil) jurisdiction in the area where the work is to be undertaken. In the case of Iberian shipwrecks, there are additional concerns of encountering human remains and material culture of high monetary value, such as bullion. The following information is based on legislative regulations in the United Kingdom at the time of writing (for general UNESCO guidelines, see Maarleveld et al. 2013). The reasons for selecting the UK as a case in point for the following discussion are twofold: 1) the UK's regulations are particularly complex, in part because it is a nation composed of four countries, each with its own standards; 2) the UK's legislation often serves as a template from which other nations compose or revise their own regulations on cultural and environmental resources. Despite the fact that the UK has not yet ratified the 2001 UNESCO Convention on the Protection of the Underwater Cultural Heritage, its national regulations for permissions, documentation, qualifications, and reporting archaeological work (and even more so for archaeological work on designated sites underwater) are strict and complicated compared to the regulations of many European and other industrialized nations (see Dromgoole 2013). Readers are encouraged to seek out current standards as they apply to their proposed place of work, even if work is to be done in the UK, as legislation regarding heritage frequently changes (see also Nautical Archaeology Society, n.d.; Bowens 2009). It is the archaeologist's responsibility to be fully aware of all legislative concerns before pursuing work on an archaeological site. Awareness of restrictions and permissions should be raised far in advance as applications can take weeks or months to be processed, and some licenses may be accompanied with fees. While the paperwork and fees may be a hassle, noncompliance would undoubtedly result in litigation and fines amounting to a great deal more paperwork and fees, not to mention a damaged reputation that could have far-reaching implications.

4.1. Heritage and environmental organizations

Under the UK's National Heritage Act of 1983, Historic England (formerly English Heritage, or the Historic Buildings and Monuments Commission of England) was established as a non-departmental public body sponsored by the Department of Culture, Media and Sport. Among other responsibilities, it supervises activities that impact cultural heritage, including archaeological excavation on land and underwater (Fenwick & Gale 1998, 147-150). In order to conduct archaeological research on a designated underwater site, Historic England requires a permit for either survey or excavation, which is granted to a licensee free of cost (Historic England 2015d [2010b]). The obligations of licensees were reinforced by the National Heritage Act of 2002 that formalized statutory responsibility of the submerged cultural heritage in England to Historic England. The licensee furnishes a complete project plan (including risk assessment; see below, 4.2.2) for activities on the site, how artefacts will be dealt with, and how the results will be disseminated (5.3; Historic England 2015b [2006]). If a permit is granted, it is valid until 30 November, after which the license must be renewed to continue work on the site. Regardless of whether or not the permit is to be renewed, Historic England also requires a licensee report by 30 November detailing the work that was done on the site, by whom and when, the status of any artefacts or samples removed from the site, analyses being undertaken, the condition of the site and its level of vulnerability, the results of the work, how it will be disseminated, and a prospectus for future work (see Historic England 2015c [2010b] and below, 4.4.).

In regards to underwater archaeology, Historic England also works closely with the Marine Management Organisation (MMO), another non-departmental public body, which was established as a result of the Marine and Coastal Access Act of 2009. As one of its remits, MMO monitors activities that impact the seabed through deposition or removal of material and includes activities such as drilling, dredging, and even burials at sea. Their current policy in regards to underwater archaeology is dependent upon whether or not power tools will be involved in excavation (Historic England 2015e [2014]). If only survey work is being done, or if sediment can be removed by hand-fanning, troweling, or shoveling, then no permit is required. If an airlift or dredge, or a chainsaw (for example), is to be used, then a marine license is required and should be produced when applying for an excavation permit from Historic England. In most cases, licenses for archaeological excavations underwater are eligible to use MMO's fast-track system, which, at this time, has a fixed fee of 175 GBP.

4.2. Approved Code of Practice (ACoP) for Scientific and Archaeological Diving Projects

The UK Health and Safety Executive (HSE) is another non-departmental public body, which emerged after the Health and Safety at Work etc. Act of 1974. HSE has generated guidelines for many different types of work conditions, and within the category of work that involves diving (**SCUBA** or **surface supply**), there are five subcategories: commercial offshore, commercial inland/inshore, media, recreational, and scientific or archaeological. The ACoP for scientific and archaeological dive operations using SCUBA outlines a set of procedures, including a chain of command, that should be followed to ensure that underwater fieldwork is in compliance with the law (Health and Safety Executive 2014 [1998]; Bowens 2009; Maarleveld et al. 2013).

The HSE also mandates that divers are in communication with surface at all times (through underwater coms or job- and lifelines), and that each diver has a minimum of two independent air supplies (two cylinders each with its own first- and second-stage regulator) in case of malfunction. Divers are 'tended' by non-diving members of the dive team who work under the watchful eye of the diving operations supervisor, who is ultimately responsible for ensuring that each diver's kit is fully functioning, that each diver is fit to dive, and that each item on the standard HSE checklist is accounted for:

1. Diver is fit to dive.
2. Harness and buoyancy control device (BCD) are secure.
3. Air is turned on.
4. If using a full-face mask, the bail-out switch-block is set to main cylinder.
5. Drysuit and/or BCD direct feed connected and working.
6. Weight belt release free and diver can find it.
7. Diver has a knife and can reach it.
8. Diver has fins, gloves, hood, mask, computer, surface marker buoy (SMB), and any other equipment necessary for the task.
9. If using a full-face mask, the bail-out test must be performed: diver must switch from main gas to bail-out and back to main gas via the switch-block.
10. Diver is secured for entry: if striding entry, tender should help diver stand and hold onto her/his cylinder until ready; if rolling, ensure water is clear for entry.
11. Coms check at designated area.

While the reader is strongly advised to seek out the analogous set of legal requirements relating to health and safety at work for her/his own locale, this section will paraphrase the ACoP's position on thorough dive planning and risk assessment.

4.2.1. Diving Project Plan

Different from the general project plan required by some heritage protection agencies, such as Historic England (see above, 4.1), the diving project plan lays out the details of diving operations, while minimizing the details of the archaeological background, significance of the work, and any top-side procedures such as recording, conservation, or dissemination. The diving project plan should break down specific underwater operations and explain how they will be achieved and how they will be supervised. In open water situations, the supervisor will not be diving and instead must maintain a two-way communication (through voice or lifelines) with the divers conducting the operation. Therefore, in the diving project plan, either the contractor or the supervisor must explain how each operation will be safely supervised by no more than one person on the surface. Each member of the diving team should have access to the plan before operations begin, and any changes to operations should be updated in the plan. The plan and its accompanying risk assessments should be ready at hand at all times while underwater work is being conducted.

4.2.2. Risk Assessments

An integral part of the diving project plan are the site- and operation-specific risk assessments and emergency safety procedures. For the general project plan (see above, 4.1), the risk assessment will be site-specific. However, for the diving project plan, this will need to be updated as necessary before each diving operation and for each site where work is to be done underwater. Risk assessments should evaluate all possible risks to those involved in boat and dive operations. Therefore, circumstances of weather, visibility, depth, breathing gases, decompression, currents, air temperature, water temperature, entanglement risks, slipping onboard, etc. should all be evaluated and rated. For the broader site risk assessment, these may be somewhat general, as weather conditions, for example, are subject to change, while visibility, currents, and entanglement on the site can be averaged or surmised. However, the operation risk assessment will be specific to the present conditions of the atmosphere, the support vessel, equipment, etc. Each risk assessment must also demonstrate ways in which risks are being mitigated, such as briefing divers on hazards, ensuring that divers are wearing exposure suits appropriate to water and weather conditions, etc.

Finally, emergency contact information must be kept up to date and in a readily accessible location. This document should include contacts (telephone, address, and radio if applicable) for coast guard, nearest decompression chambers, local doctors and hospitals, police, and any other relevant sources for emergency assistance.

4.3. Receiver of Wreck

The Receiver of Wreck (RoW) is a government official who addresses the treatment of wreck and salvage operations as delimited by the Merchant Shipping Act of 1995. Besides the UK, Canada and Ireland also have a receiver of wreck, and other countries may have similar posts or agencies that interpret federal or local salvage laws on behalf of finders and owners.

Under UK law, 'wreck' can be considered:

> *Flotsam*: floating goods lost from a perished ship that can be recovered on the surface of the water;
> *Jetsam*: goods cast overboard from a ship in danger of sinking without the intent of later recovery;
> *Derelict*: property (goods or the entire vessel) abandoned at sea without the intent of later recovery;
> *Lagan*: goods cast overboard in a manner such that the owner could retrieve them at a later time.

Any items falling into these categories, regardless of size or significance, and landed in the UK must be reported to the RoW, even if the finder and owner are the same entity. The fine for not reporting items is up to 2500 GBP. In the UK, reported items may not be removed from the country for one year, nor may they be destroyed or sold. During this one-year period, the RoW may conduct an investigation into the ownership of the wreck, and the owner may step forward at this time to present a title of ownership to the RoW. Unclaimed wreck is handed over to the Crown after one year, unless the find was made outside UK territory, in which case the unclaimed wreck is handed over to the finder as salvage (see: JNAPC 2007; https://www.gov.uk/report-wreck-material).

4.4. Follow-up reports and archiving

Archiving is necessary because it allows primary source information to become available for public consultation, which is only fair and just since many archaeological investigations are managed through the awardance of public funds. Furthermore, complete public access to data and scientific transparency allow for alternative interpretations to be made. For archaeological data, archived material should include any scientific or otherwise quantitative results to come out of archaeological fieldwork (Niven & Pierce-McManamon 2011; Bowens 2009). Licensee reports submitted to Historic England (see above, 4.1) are archived in the Historic England Archive. Other pieces of archive deposited with HE are available to view free of cost, or for a modest fee to download from the organization's website or to receive a print copy. Other kinds of follow-up reports may be required from funding organizations. In all cases, the outline of the final report should include a project background, objectives, methods, results, prospectus for future work, and bibliography; however, each entity requesting a report will have its own requirements, and in many cases, a template may be provided or requested to make sure that all reporting standards are met. Licensee reports are incorporated nationally, in the case of England, in the National Record on the Historic Environment and should also be deposited in the local National Environment Records (HERs) where the archaeological work is being done. Besides ensuring public access, keeping HERs up to date ensures that local authorities are aware of the heritage that may be at risk by development.

Researchers working outside the UK should check with that country's respective heritage agency to learn about the standard procedures for archiving data and their requirements. To assist in this task, the Archaeology Data Service (ADS) in the UK and Digital Antiquity in the US have collaborated to provide a set of general guidelines for ensuring the archival quality of digital documents produced during archaeological fieldwork (Niven & Pierce-McManamon 2007).

Archiving standards for archaeology have been compiled elsewhere as well (Brown 2011 [2007]; ARCHES 2007-2013) to include non-digital records, such as licenses, maps, logbooks, drawings, plans, film and slide photographs, etc. For underwater archaeology, dive logs are also an essential part of the archive.

When dealing with samples, the sample itself as well as the results of analyses undertaken will also become part of the site archive. Therefore, there will need to be an arrangement made with an appropriate archiving and/or conservation facility for how and where the samples will be stored after analysis, assuming non-destructive methods are used or there are remaining materials after destructive analyses are conducted. Projects should discuss the plans for longer-term sample storage, reburial, conservation, or even disposal, with the relevant analytical and conservation laboratories. In the case of shipwreck assemblages that are being conserved, samples can be used as part of wood condition assessments before being integrated into the hull conservation program.

For the results of scientific analyses that may be conducted for **dendroprovenance** (Figure 5; 2.1, 3.3), there are international databanks available for tree-ring studies and most recently, some stable **isotope** analyses. The most commonly used databank for dendrochronology is the International Tree-Ring Data Bank (ITRDB) which is hosted by the US National Oceanic and Atmospheric Administration (NOAA). All tree-ring data and metadata may be stored here free of charge and is likewise freely available to researchers worldwide. Recently, efforts have been undertaken to include isotope data, particularly carbon-13 and oxygen-18, in the metadata of tree-rings. TRiDaS is an independent database and represents another option for the deposition of standardized tree-ring data and metadata that can be read universally (Brewer & Jansma 2015). Besides tree-rings, there are also several genome databanks, the most inclusive being GenBank, which represents a vast open access repository for DNA sequences of all types of organisms, including plants. GenBank and the related databank Genome are both maintained by the US National Center for Biotechnology Information (NCBI).

Chapter 5
Ethical Considerations

Aside from the far-reaching legalities involved with shipwreck archaeology (see Chapter 4), which are dependent on local and federal legislation, ethical considerations apply more universally. They may not be governed by laws, and noncompliance may not be punishable with fines, but abiding by the set of guidelines presented below will help to ensure that the irreplaceable heritage that shipwrecks represent is treated with the respect that it deserves. While the sale of antiquities is discussed above (1.4), this section will discuss issues of *in-situ* preservation, maintaining site 'authenticity', archaeology as a destructive science, and the importance of dissemination (especially open-access) in maritime archaeology.

5.1. UNESCO and *in-situ* preservation

The 2001 UNESCO Convention for the Protection of the Underwater Cultural Heritage (UCH) recommends *in-situ* preservation as first recourse (see: www.unesco.org). The reason for discouraging unnecessary surfacing of cultural heritage results from three main lines of thought:

- Laboratory treatment of waterlogged elements may be expensive and time consuming, while a risk of deterioration of material always remains.
- Museum buildings often lack room and conditions to accommodate large wooden or metallic objects recovered from wrecks.
- The authenticity of a site, its context, and its integrity cannot be guaranteed when objects are recovered.

However, the Convention acknowledges that leaving heritage assets *in situ* is not always the best course of action (or non-action, as the case may be). Recovery of artifacts or even entire vessels can be justified if doing so would make a 'significant contribution to protection or knowledge or enhancement of underwater cultural heritage' (Rule 1; see Maarleveld et al. 2013, 21). What constitutes a 'significant contribution' is highly subjective, but the following three scenarios are provided:

- the underwater cultural heritage remains are threatened by any natural or human factors (i.e., urban and port developments, pillage, environmental conditions, etc.);
- scientific research can obtain results that contribute significantly to the knowledge of the history of humanity;
- study, research, and dissemination enhance the awareness and consideration of a region towards the protection of its underwater cultural heritage.

The second scenario applies most directly to any archaeological campaign with a focus on *in-situ* timber sampling for provenance. However, in many cases, two or even all three scenarios could apply to intended investigations on a shipwreck. As mentioned above (3.1.1), the seafloor is a dynamic place, and in areas subject to intense anthro-, geo-, or biogenic changes, wooden ship remains are frequently at greater risk for loss or irreparable damage (Björdal & Gregory 2011). Additionally, because 'Iberian' shipwrecks are found all over the world, a shipwreck excavation or sampling campaign could be a rare chance to raise awareness of submerged heritage in places that may not have major public museums, like the *Vasa* or the *Mary Rose*, devoted to maritime heritage (see 5.3). Before removing any material from a site, these factors – complex and subjective though they may be – should be taken into consideration and applied to the site under discussion. Each is unique, and therefore, each must be considered in light of its own circumstances above and below the waves.

At the same time, UNESCO regulations for UCH make clear that even scientific activities 'shall not adversely affect the underwater cultural heritage more than is necessary for the objectives of the project' (Maarleveld et al. 2013, 37, rule 3). In order to ensure that the impact of scientific activities is proportional to the potential knowledge gained,

> A cautious step-by-step approach and phased decision-making may be the best way to avoid disproportional impact. Due to the constraints of proportionality of impact, archaeological research is continually caught between sampling strategies and total excavation. In order for science to progress, a combination of both strategies is needed. Sampling and excavation are complementary. One is not necessarily less radical than the other. Sampling the construction of a ship's hull for example, is extremely radical. It is perhaps more radical than a total excavation in which a hull is left intact, because that is deemed more 'consistent with protection'. Such sampling is not necessarily less proportionate or responsible, however, as it also yields other information. (Maarleveld et al. 2013, 39)

In sampling a site's timbers, the information gained can include fundamental data, like dates and provenance, but ring widths, DNA, and isotopic data from wood samples can also contribute to ongoing studies of global concern. A shipwreck's well preserved timber assemblage is an archive, not only of historic shipbuilding and carpentry, but also of climatic fluctuations, forestry practices and international trade that can cast light on broad socio-environmental changes. Likewise, older shipwrecks and submerged forests can help develop long-term Holocene climate records and determine how plant and human species reacted to rapidly rising sea levels, an issue which is again of concern today as we face unprecedented levels of global warming and sea-level rise (Rich et al., in press). Clearly, the potential data gained from sampling may indeed be proportional to the destructive impact or act of displacement. That being said, the potential for obtaining these data must still be weighed against the potential for irreversible damage to shipwrecks as unique and vulnerable aspects of cultural heritage.

5.2. Destruction or displacement?

As stated above (5.1), UNESCO's third reason for encouraging *in-situ* preservation claims that, 'The authenticity of a site, its context and its integrity cannot be guaranteed when objects are recovered from it.' With the removal of wood samples from a shipwreck, or other artefacts of the assemblage, the site is changed permanently. While most archaeologists readily admit that ours is a destructive science, alternatively, we can think about sampling procedures less as destruction, and more as displacement (Lucas 2001). All intrusive fieldwork, whether ethnography, biology, geology, or archaeology, results in destroying the very things we are trying to understand. This sentiment of loss that accompanies the paradox of fieldwork stems from a basic understanding of the process as one of the disturbance of authenticity, integrity, or 'purity' (Lucas 2001, 2012). If we can reroute that thinking to understand this change of context as a productive rather than reductive one, then we can also see artefacts as objects existing in phases of context. As an object experiences displacement from one context, it experiences placement into another, so that archaeological practice becomes a creative act as much as a destructive one.

With wood samples, this idea of displacement can be attested by considering those that are removed, measured, and then conserved, and to an even greater degree those that are removed, measured, and then replaced *in situ*. However, this line of thinking becomes slightly more complicated with wood samples submitted to destructive analytical processes, such as **mass spectrometry**. Traditional thought would claim that the processes of taking and analysing samples destroys both context and artefact. If that were completely true though, then the researcher would be left with nothing, and we know from practice that this is not the case. The artefact's context is altered, and rather than the object experiencing annihilation, its physical matter is likewise converted into quantifiable data, which is then subject to interpretation – again, creating new contexts (and new meanings) through various acts of displacement. This is perhaps a helpful way of thinking about sampling procedures: that is, while we have clear obligations for maintaining the primary source data, the processes of obtaining these data are not fundamentally inauthentic or impure.

5.3. Dissemination

Regardless of whether or not one prefers to think of archaeology, and archaeological sampling in particular, as destruction or displacement (or in another way altogether), disseminating our research questions, methods, and results is imperative (Bowens 2009). In accordance with standard deontological practice (see 1.4), scientific researchers are responsible for publishing their studies in a timely manner because knowledge builds on previously produced knowledge. Without rigorous scientific research and the publication thereof, knowledge stagnates. Other scientists as well as the general public share professional and personal interests in what archaeologists do. This is no less the case with shipwrecks, which are a subject of popular fascination the world round. However, underwater archaeology poses something of a challenge to effective dissemination, especially to the public.

The nature of underwater archaeology is closed off to most people. Even sport divers have limited access to underwater sites, due to depth or other physical conditions, or due to the licensing requirements for accessing protected sites. The most commonly visited shipwrecks are the ones that have been brought to the surface (*Vasa*, the *Mary Rose*). Other vessels, such as the Newport Ship or Khufu's Solar Barge, were never wrecked *per se* but have also been made available to the public through the opening of their own museum. This of course, is not possible in all cases, nor is it even encouraged in most cases (5.1).

Even so, there are some effective examples of *in-situ* preservation in combination with public dissemination. Shipwrecks in Lake Michigan (US) rest in water clear enough that tourists can see the wrecks from glass-bottomed tour boats. Of course, this experience of a site is somewhat fleeting, and furthermore, it only works for shallow sites in clear water; deeper wreck sites or those in murky waters would remain unavailable. **Dive trails** are another good example of how the UNESCO convention can be followed while opening up submerged heritage to the diving public. For example, a dive trail off the coast of Galicia (Spain) includes shipwrecks divable on **SCUBA** that range from galleons to submarines. The Spanish Plate Fleet wrecked along the Florida Keys (US) in 1733 presents another case for how Iberian vessels comprising a single wrecking event have been presented to diving communities concerned with heritage, instructed to 'take only photos and leave only bubbles.' However, the vast majority of people, even those with a vested interest in maritime heritage, do not dive. Modern technology can provide a way to combine *in-situ* preservation with dissemination to the public, diving or not.

3D models can be made through **photogrammetry** (for photogrammetry as a way to record excavation, see: Demesticha et al. 2014), which can then be uploaded onto web-based platforms, such as Sketchfab, accessible by everyone with a reasonably fast internet connection. The advantage of a 3D model, as opposed to a **photomosaic**, is that the audience has a greater chance to interact with the site. Viewers can 'swim' around features such as canons, concretions, and combustion engines, exploring even fine details for themselves. The 3D model of the wrecked galleon in the Eo Estuary at Ribadeo (Galicia, Spain) provides a good example of this (Figure 22; https://skfb.ly/HF8R). The integration of gaming software with a 3D model can also allow for a more inclusive participant experience, as exemplified by ArtasMedia's virtual **dive trail** consisting of three twentieth-century British shipwreck sites (https://artasmedia.com/project-tag/historic-england/).

Another technological step toward allowing viewers a **dry dive** on the site is through **virtual reality**. Web-based software applications can create the effect of 'being' underwater, thereby giving audience members a more realistic experience of interacting with their underwater heritage. VR applications can begin with an exceptional **photogrammetry** model, as can be seen in the example of the British Admiralty steam drifter HMD John Mitchell (https://skfb.ly/FBHN). Eventually **augmented reality** technologies incorporating holograms could be used as well. At this point in their development, both of these methods champion the so-called 'primacy of vision', so more democratic methods

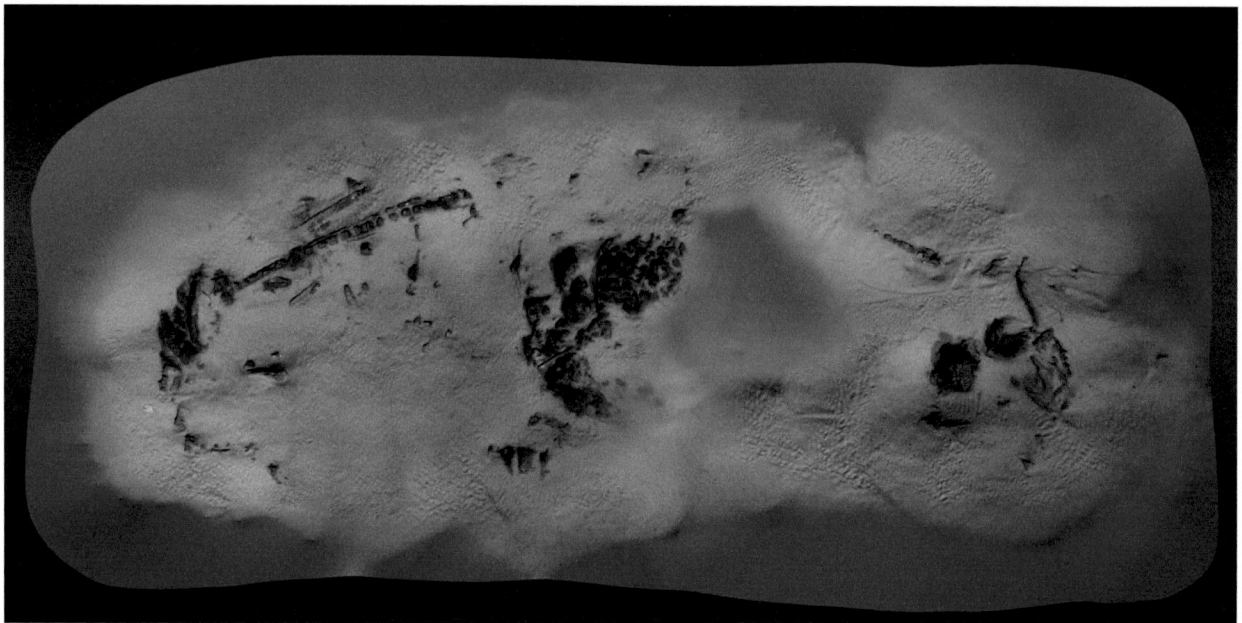

Figure 22. 2D image of the 3D site model produced through photogrammetry of the wrecked sixteenth-century galleon at Ribadeo (Galicia, Spain), hosted on Sketchfab. Model by Brandon Mason, ©Maritime Archaeology Ltd., 2015.

of dissemination could seek to appeal to other senses beyond only sight to develop a multi-sensory experience. Augmented reality promises to do just that as its next development will likely be meta-sensory engagement in the form of direct brain-computer interface.

In a much more traditional vein, involving local press and filmmakers can result in documentaries of the research on a site, which are highly attractive to the public. Documentaries can be uploaded to YouTube or other video hosting websites, and links can be made through social media, departmental or site web pages, or the project blog.

Although somewhat time-consuming, blogging can also be an effective way to engage the public and peers with ongoing project research. Interdisciplinary efforts will not go unnoticed, and blogs can highlight site work that extends beyond archaeology to include historical archive research, experimental components, visual recording, cross-cultural encounters, software engineering, specialist analyses, conservation efforts, and ecological awareness to name a few. One example of an interdisciplinary approach to project blogging can be found at https://forseadiscovery.wordpress.com/.

Although perhaps not the most exciting method of dissemination, complete archiving is another important way of ensuring that work on a site, any materials lifted, results of analyses, and conclusions are made available to peers and the public, and that this primary source information is available for perpetuity as well (see also 4.4).

Despite the fundamentally inaccessible nature of most shipwrecks, options for disseminating even underwater archaeology are limited only by the creativity of the researchers involved. Even with limited time and budgets, there are innumerable innovative ways to bring *in-situ* shipwrecks to the surface, so to speak, in order to foster greater public awareness of and appreciation for the fleets beneath the seas.

Chapter 6
Conclusions

As we find ourselves again submerged in an era of radical, rapid change, it is crucial to understand how those who came before us either succumbed to or overcame their own periods of war, state power fluctuations, socio-economic circumstances, phases of human depopulation and overpopulation, deforestation, climate anomalies, and rising sea levels. Studying shipwreck timbers can provide us with this very information on past socio-environmental policy and practice. As mentioned above, a small piece of a wrecked ship's timber is much more than a soggy old bit of wood. It is an archive to be read, interpreted, and applied. By tracing the wood sampled back to its parent tree and original forest environment, we place ourselves in a better situation to grasp and responsibly control the relationships between the human race and the rest of our shared planet. Maritime history is a history of humanity's place in the world – colonization, exploitation, cooperation, technological revolutions – and this history is structuring our present and will continue to predict our future.

Environmental historians have demonstrated that the fundamentally close relationship between human societies and natural resources can be characterized by phases of cooperation, competition, and exploitation. The interplay between innovation and technological changes in shipbuilding throughout time, but especially in the Early Modern era, is a function of this relationship, particularly as it has negotiated the scarcity – either real or perceived – of timber. Historical and archaeological discourses have focused on forest-human relationships and emphasized the importance of wood as an indisputably valuable raw material for the construction of navies and merchant fleets (Perlin 1989; Richards 2006; Rich 2017). However, this indisputable value can really only be assessed fully through interdisciplinary studies that include history and archaeology, but also wood science.

6.1. Future of scientific and maritime archaeologies

As demonstrated in the above text, nautical archaeology involving a strategic timber sampling campaign for **dendroprovenance** (or dating) can create several different avenues for combining shipwreck archaeology and archaeological sciences. With new methods for determining wood provenance being developed all the time, and established ones working steadily towards greater accuracy and precision, the future of dendroprovenance is bright. Non-invasive techniques using CT scanning for ring measurement and species ID have also been developed (Bill et al. 2012; Stelzner & Million 2015), and although this method has no underwater application yet, it seems that many lab-based technologies are currently being adapted for use in underwater fieldwork. Nautical archaeology has seen great advances in technology in recent years, including the use of acoustic and photographic mapping techniques, underwater GPS, tablets adapted for underwater use, ROVs, and even specialized aquanaut suits for excavating deepwater wrecks. Underwater drones or other robotics-based engineering could be the next major technological advancement applied to archaeology underwater. And countless other innovations are on the way, some of which we can't even imagine yet. This is truly an exciting time for archaeologists and for archaeology.

Training more underwater archaeologists in scientific specializations, and wood scientists in doing archaeology underwater, will help ensure that communications between the multiple brackets of archaeology remain open and productive (Jones 2004). This is not to say that specialist status is easy to come by, but having an idea of what it takes to extract and amplify DNA from a piece of wood, or what it takes to remove that piece of wood from the underwater environment, will lend perspective and foster mutual understanding of work conditions and the amount of effort that goes into producing results. This can only result in greater cooperation and communication between departments with ultimately similar aims.

6.2. Importance of inter- and multi-disciplinary collaboration

Along these same lines, going beyond archaeology is increasingly important to gain a more robust understanding of the past, and by extension, the present and future. Inter- and multi-disciplinary collaboration is essential to maximizing the informational potential of a site. While often used interchangeably, these two terms have subtle but important differences in meaning. Interdisciplinary refers to collaborations that involve several disciplinary approaches to create a unified story. Multi-discplinary collaborations involve several disciplinary approaches to create a variety of stories about the same subject. Both approaches can be used within the same project. By examining the same subject from as many different angles as possible, a consensus is all the more likely. And even if a consensus is never reached, say for example, on the provenance of a certain shipwreck, the differences in results and conclusions incite the kind of debate that stimulates still further research, which in turn, refines the methods available for use and even the questions able to be asked.

As explained in the previous chapters, for the determination of timber provenance, nautical archaeologists should work closely with wood, forestry, and even carpentry experts (e.g., Crumlin-Pedersen 1995; Croome 1999). In the case of Iberian 'Age of Discovery' shipwrecks, collaborating with wood scientists along with historians and art historians has proved vital to gaining a fuller understanding

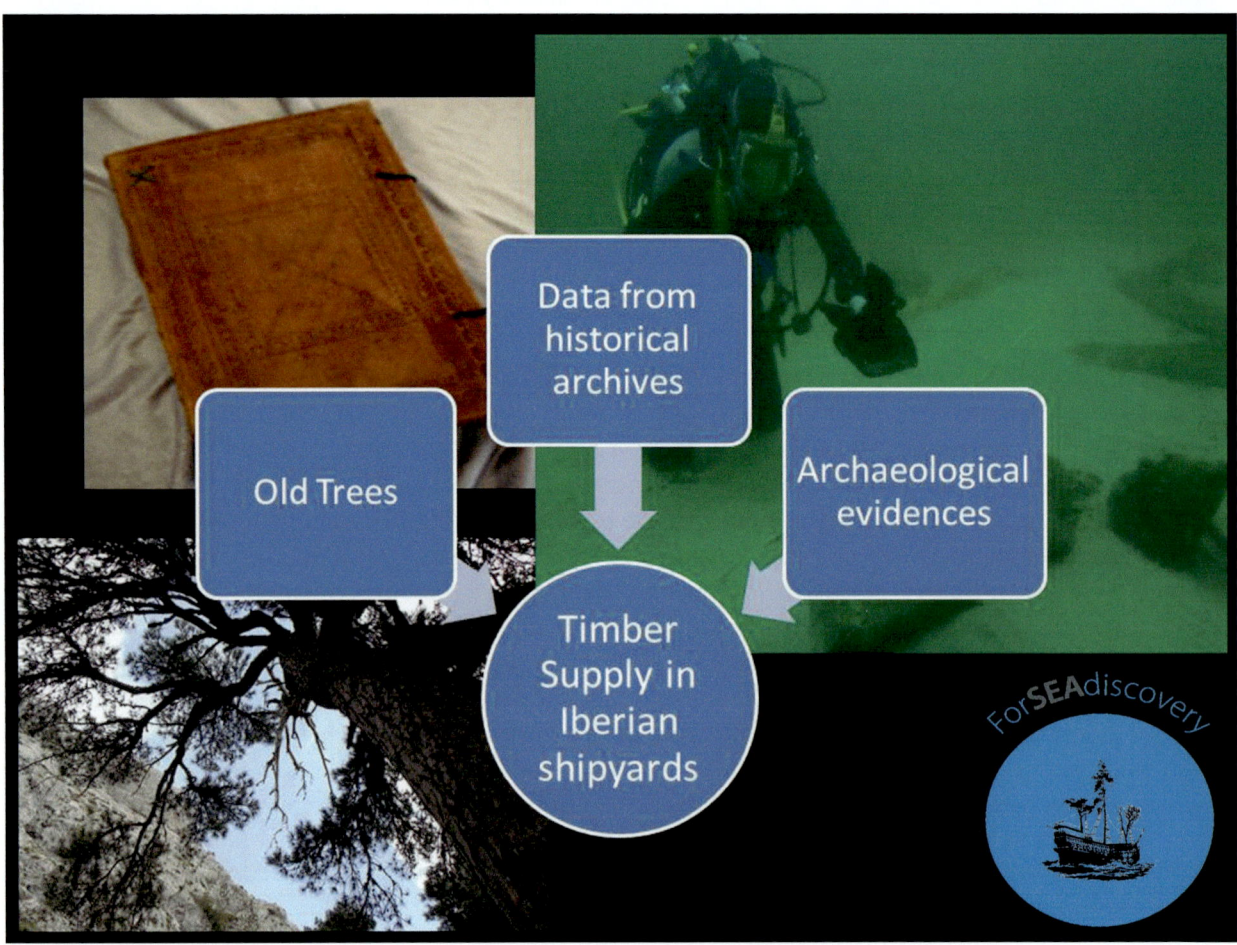

FIGURE 23. EXAMPLE OF AN INTER- AND MULTI-DISCIPLINARY WORK FLOW, AS MODELED BY THE FORSEADISCOVERY PROJECT, WHICH AIMS TO ELUCIDATE IBERIAN TIMBER TRADE FOR SHIPBUILDING AND THE EFFECTS OF SHIPBUILDING ON DEFORESTATION IN THE PENINSULA DURING THE AGE OF DISCOVERY. IMAGE © ANA CRESPO SOLANA.

of shipbuilding, timber trade, forestry, and shipyard activity, as evidenced in archives of tree rings, historical documents, and shipwreck assemblages (Figure 23; Crespo Solana & Nayling 2016; Trindade et al. in press; Crespo Solana 2015; Martin 2000, 2001; Casabán 2017). In several cases, shipwrecks have been tentatively identified by name, and historical information on the construction, wrecking event, the crew, and the cargo has been elaborated. As with most intellectual pursuits, multiple heads and hands working together generate the most robust theories.

Glossary

Annual growth rings: rings visible on the **transverse** section formed by many tree types on an annual basis. They are characterized by early-wood growth, which appears lighter in color and may be characterized by pores (as in ring-porous and semi-porous species), and late-wood growth, which appears darker in color with smaller, denser cells. A growth ring indicates the amount of wood produced by the cambium during one growing season, which notably, is not always equivalent to one year.

Archaeometry: application of physical and biological scientific techniques to analyse or measure elements of ancient art, artefacts, and materials. Archaeometric methods are used in dating, provenancing, remote sensing, and conserving, as well as in mathematical methods and **environmental history**.

Augmented reality: a digital technology that creates a composite view of reality by superimposing a computer-generated image, like a hologram, on a user's view of the real world.

Carbohydrates: chemical compounds composed of carbon, hydrogen, and oxygen that provide cells with energy. Carbohydrates come in the form of sugars, starches, and **cellulose**.

Cellulose: organic compound (polysaccharide, or polymer consisting of chains of bonded sugars) that is the chief instrument in the cell walls of plants and other living organisms. Cellulose is found in the wood, bark, roots, and leaves of plants, and it is insoluble in water. Because cellulose is the primary organic component of wood, cellulose is the most abundant variety of organic compound.

Chloroplast DNA: abbreviated cpDNA, chloroplasts are sub-cellular units in plants and algae with their own DNA that may be used in the **DNA barcoding** of tree species. While mitochondrial DNA (mtDNA) is used to identify animals, cpDNA is the preferred genome target for plants.

Coniferous: in botany, trees and shrubs that bear cones and are classified as gymnosperms. Most (with the exception of larch, which is **deciduous**, are evergreen and do not annually shed their foliage. Many evergreen trees are not coniferous, however: e.g., eucalyptus, holly, and live oak. Deciduous evergreens tend to be **hardwoods**, while conifers are **softwoods**.

Conversion: the act of converting a tree into usable lumber, whether by ax, adze, or saw. Conversion, especially of planks and boards, is often either **radial** or **tangential**.

Core sample: a narrow cylindrical sample (of, e.g., rock, sediment, ice, or wood) removed with a type of drill. Core samples of wood are taken with an **increment borer** and usually feature the **radial** growth of the **transverse** section of a tree, ideally from the **pith** to the bark. Core samples can be removed from living trees without harm.

Cross-dating: statistical comparison of a tree-ring sequence against a **master regional chronology** to determine the date of the sample and its approximate location at the time of felling.

Cross-section: a flat cylindrical sample that features the entire **transverse** section of a tree, offering the full record of the tree's growth as opposed to the partial view offered by a **core sample**. Cross-sections must be obtained by felling the tree or removing the sample from a tree that has already been felled. Cross sections from archaeological materials are taken ideally from the ends of timbers to avoid compromising the structure.

^{14}C wiggle matching: a method of dating a wood sample when **cross-dating** is not possible. The radiocarbon calibration curve was constructed to convert radiocarbon years into calendar years by testing results against securely-dated **annual growth rings** of long-lived bristlecone pines. Wiggle-matching compares samples with many years of growth against the 'wiggles' of the radiocarbon calibration curve, which can provide a date range that is more precise than radiocarbon alone.

Deciduous: in botany, trees and shrubs (most of which are classified as angiosperms) that lose their leaves annually and remain leafless for some time: winter in temperate forests and during the dry season in tropical and subtropical forests. Deciduous trees in temperate and boreal broadleaf forests correspond with **hardwoods** like oak and maple; in tropical and subtropical forests, with hardwoods like teak and mahogany.

Dendroprovenance: determination of the provenance of wood, particularly as it pertains to ancient wooden objects or materials.

Deontology: the study of the nature of duty and obligation, particularly as it pertains to work ethics and the morality of actions: namely, that the action itself should be right (moral, ethical) regardless of the consequences of the action.

Dive trail: established underwater trail that leads recreational divers on a tour of underwater cultural heritage sites, including shipwrecks, which may also function as marine sanctuaries. Trails may be monitored by heritage agencies or other stakeholders.

DNA barcoding: various methods of amplifying DNA sequences to identify species based on genetic variability and unique genetic qualities. This method is different from DNA fingerprinting, which identifies individuals, clones, and lineages.

Dry dive: traditionally referring to experiencing the effects of breathing compressed air at depth in a hyperbaric chamber, the term is now also used for various digital technologies (e.g., virtual reality) that allow people to visit underwater sites virtually; hence in this usage, it is synonymous with 'virtual dive'.

Environmental history: the study of interactions between humans and the non-human and non-anthropogenic worlds over time, and how both have played active roles in the development of human history.

FTIR: Fourier Transform Infrared spectroscopy is a chemical measurement technique that generates an infrared spectrum of a sample by plotting infrared light output as a function of infrared wavelength. The spectrum reflects molecular bond vibrations and atomic masses through respective amounts of infrared absorption. It can be used to determine the chemical and molecular compositions of organic and inorganic materials.

Hardwood: wood from angiosperms, or broadleaved and evergreen **deciduous** trees.

Heartwood: older center-most part of the stem that functions only to maintain the tree's stability. It was once **sapwood** that has been decommissioned but has developed chemical resistances to decay and rot; therefore, heartwood is encountered in construction projects, such as shipbuilding, where the rest of the **xylem** was often removed.

Increment borer: instrument used to extract wood from living and felled trees and historical and archaeological wooden objects. It consists of a cylindrical handle that holds an auger and extractor tray. When taken apart, the auger, a kind of hollow drill, is positioned perpendicular to the handle and locked in, and then screwed into the tree or non-living wood. When the auger is penetrated sufficiently deep into the wood, the extractor tray is slipped into the auger, between it and the wood inside it. The auger is then unscrewed and the extractor tray pulled out with the **core sample** resting on top.

Isotope: form of a chemical element that contains different numbers of neutrons but the same number of protons; in other words, every atom of a given element may have a range of numbers of neutrons. So while the atomic number remains the same (as it is dependent upon the number of protons, which is equal to the number of electrons in a neutral atom), the mass number of an isotope is different because it is the sum of the number of protons (atomic number) and the variable number of neutrons. Isotopes can be stable (e.g. ^{13}C, which has six protons and seven neutrons) or radioactive (e.g., ^{14}C, which has six protons and eight neutrons).

Lignin: a class of molecularly variable organic polymers (defined as a dendritic network polymer of phenyl propene basic units) that bind cells, fibers, and vessels that make up wood and the woody tissues of vascular plants and some algae. Lignin provides structure to cell walls, and with its resistance to water solubility, it is vital in the conduction of water through the stem.

Maritime archaeology: the archaeological discipline that focuses on human activities and material culture related to waterways (marine, estuarine, lacustrine, and riverine), including ships and boats, coastal installations, dams and mills, fishing and shellfishing industries, submerged landscapes, etc. It may be compared with **underwater archaeology** and **nautical archaeology**.

Mass spectrometry: analytical technique that measures the masses of particles and molecules and their structure, and the sample's elemental and isotopic signature, by generating a mass spectrum, or an intensity plot of the ion signal as a function of the mass-to-charge ratio. The sample must first be ionized, which may occur through repeated exposure to or bombardment of electrons. Often used in archaeological applications, inductively coupled plasma mass spectrometry (ICP-MS) produces a plasma from argon gas that is first ionized by high temperatures before ionizing the sample in turn. Then the ions of the sample are separated quantified with the mass spectrometer.

Master regional chronology: a series of averaged tree-ring chronologies that define the growth patterns of a specific tree species in a specific region over a long period of time. The master regional chronology is used in dendrochronological **cross-dating**.

Nautical archaeology: archaeological discipline that studies ships and boats, including their construction, architecture, propulsion, functions, evolution, wrecking events, abandonment, deposition processes, and conservation. May be compared with **maritime archaeology** and **underwater archaeology**.

Palynology: the study of pollen grains and other kinds of spores (including fungal, algal, and protozoan), often from sedimentary deposits, and particularly as they pertain to long-term regional vegetation history.

Photogrammetry: photographic application for survey and mapping that allows for distances between objects to be measured accurately. After calibration and determination of the relative position and orientation of the camera for each photo relative to the subject, a 3D point cloud can be generated of matching locations. Dense point clouds are then used to build a geometrical mesh, from which a texture map is calculated and applied to the 3D geometry, which can then be used for measurements, visualization, or 3D printing.

Photomosaic: series of overlapping photographs of a single locale that are stitched together at areas of overlap to create a larger picture plane. A photomosaic may encompass a large geographical area (as in satellite imagery) or a smaller site that is still beyond the scope of a single photograph.

Pith: the central tissue composing the stem of vascular plants. In trees, the pith is the center-most ring of growth surrounded by layers of **xylem**, first **heartwood** then **sapwood**, before being surrounded by the cambium and then the phloem, or bark.

Polymerase chain reaction: abbreviated PCR, this technique selects and amplifies as little as a single copy of a DNA sequence to generate up to millions of copies enabling the analysis of very small amounts of sample for the purpose of **DNA barcoding** and fingerprinting.

Py-GC/MS: pyrolysis-gas chromatography-mass spectrometry is a technique that targets insoluble components with high molecular mass by heating in a pyrolyzer to cleave the molecular structure, whose moieties indicate the types of macromolecules in the sample. The pyrolyzates are then further separated through gas chromatography and quantified through **mass spectrometry** to identify the chemical composition of the sample.

Radial: in wood, a longitudinal section of the stem where the section is parallel to the radius of the stem. Radial **conversion** of wood refers to timber cut parallel to the radius of the circular growth pattern of the tree.

Raking light: illumination from a light source at an angle that is oblique or parallel to the subject in order to better see or photograph surface textures.

Resin: combinations of organic compounds that are insoluble in water and can be solid or viscous in nature. They are produced by woody plants to seal and protect the plant from insect or pathogen invasion following an injury. They can be converted into polymers.

Sample population: also referred to as the experimentally accessible population, it is the population to be sampled, which is typically much smaller than the **target population**.

Sapwood: most recent wood produced by the tree's cambium (the only living part of the stem) that still has an active role in conducting water through the stem from roots to leaves, and seasonally returning energy back to the roots. Sapwood is the most **resinous** part of the **xylem** and often has some fragrant and even pesticidal properties.

Scantlings: Standard dimensions for the parts a ship's structure or especially any given ship timber element.

SCUBA: an acronym for a self-contained underwater breathing apparatus that is independent of air supplies at the surface. Methods of scuba include variations on open-circuit (exhaled or otherwise discharged gas is released into the ambient environment) and closed-circuit rebreather (discharged gas is reclaimed and re-breathed).

Softwood: wood from **coniferous** trees, or gymnosperms.

Surface supply: method of diving where diver's air supply is pumped down through an umbilical hose from the surface, usually from onboard a support vessel but optionally from the shore. The air-filled umbilical enters the diver's helmet or full-face mask. Air supply in helmets can be free-flowing or demand-based, while masks employ only demand valves. Both helmets and masks come in open-circuit (exhaled or otherwise discharged gas is released into the ambient environment) and closed-circuit rebreather (discharged gas is reclaimed and re-breathed) varieties.

Tangential: in wood, a longitudinal section of a stem where the section is perpendicular to the radius of the stem. Tangential **conversion** of wood refers to timber cut tangentially to the circular growth pattern of the tree.

Tannin: a water-soluble organic compound with astringent properties found in leaf, bud, seed, root, and stem tissues in **hardwoods** and **softwoods** (more in the former than in the latter). Tannins may help regulate tissue growth, and their astringency may function as a pesticide while abating predation.

Target population: population about which information in sought, but which in most statistical analyses, is too great to sample due to restrictions of time, budget, and other resources, which leads researchers to select a subset of the target, or the **sample population**.

Teredo gallery: calcareous tunnels made by the wood-boring mollusk, teredo, that serve as the animal's burrow.

Trace elements: chemical elements with very low concentrations in a material (often expressed in parts per million (ppm)), which can be measured by **mass spectrometry** or other **archaeometric** techniques. Archaeological applications include nutrition and provenance (or material source) studies.

Transverse: a **cross-section** that slices horizontally through the longitudinal axis of a specimen; in trees, a horizontal plane that intersects the stem perpendicularly.

Underwater archaeology: branch of archaeology that is practiced underwater. Studies may include submerged wreck sites of ships and airplanes, disposal sites such as cargo dumps, submerged landscapes, sacrificial sites such as cenotes, submerged port- and harbor-related structures, and any other aspect of material culture or human activity located on the beds of seas, lakes, rivers, and estuaries. May be compared with **maritime archaeology** and **nautical archaeology**.

Virtual reality: abbreviated VR, a digital technology that uses a headset to simulate an environment and the user's physical presence in this environment.

Waney edge: also called the bark edge, this is the part of a converted piece of timber that retains traces of the phloem (bark), and therefore, the last growth period (year or season) before the tree was felled. Depending on the lumber's qualities, its **conversion**, and its function, the waney edge may be found on timbers whose **sapwood** was not entirely stripped away.

Xylem: the woody part of a tree, including **sapwood** and **heartwood**, that lies behind the phloem, or bark.

Xylophagic: referring to organisms that eat wood, such as termites and engraver beetles on land, or teredo, piddock, and gribble in underwater.

Bibliography

Agius, D. A. 2008. *Classic Ships of Islam: From Mesopotamia to the Indian Ocean.* Leiden, Brill.

Ahlström, C. 1997. *Looking for Leads. Shipwrecks of the Past Revealed by Contemporary Documents and the Archaeological Record.* Helsinki, The Finnish Academy of Science and Letters.

Allevato, E., Ermolli, E. R. and de Pasquale, G. 2009. Woodland exploitation and Roman shipbuilding: Preliminary data from the shipwreck Napoli C (Naples, Italy). *Méditeranée* 112: 33-42.

ARCHES. 2015. *A Standard and Guide to Best Practice for Archaeological Archiving in Europe.* Prepared by K. Perrin, D. H. Brown, G. Lange, D. Bibby, A. Carlsson, A. Degraeve, M. Kuna, Y. Larsson, S. U. Pálsdóttir, B. Stoll-Tucker, C. Dunning, A. R. von Bieberstein. EAC Guidelines 1. Namur: Europae Archaeologia Consilium. http://archaeologydataservice.ac.uk/arches/Wiki.jsp?page=The%20Standard%20and%20Guide%20to%20Best%20Practice%20in%20Archaeological%20Archiving%20in%20Europe. Last accessed on 20 July 2017.

Apestegui, C. 1998. La arquitectura naval entre 1660 y 1754. Aproximación a los aspectos tecnológicos y su reflejo en la construcción en Guipúzcoa. *Itsas Memoria. Revista de Estudios Marítimios del País Vasco,* 2: 267-295. Donostia - San Sebastian, Untzi Museoa - Museo Naval.

Barnes, A. 2011. *Close-Range Photogrammetry: A Guide to Good Practice.* Archaeological Data Service / Digital Antiquity: Guides to Good Practice: http://guides.archaeologydataservice.ac.uk/g2gp/Photogram_Toc. Last accessed 20 July 2017.

Beuchot, M. 1997. The philosophical discussion of the legitimacy of the conquest of Mexico in the sixteenth century. Translated by C. Abellán. In K. White (ed.), *Hispanic Philosophy in the Age of Discovery*: 31-44. Studies in Philospy and the History of Philosophy, volume 29. Washington D.C., Catholic University of America Press.

Bill, J., Daly, A., Johnsen, Ø., and Dalen, K. S. 2012. DendroCT – Dendrochronology without the damage. *Dendrochronologia* 30: 223-230.

Birch, S. and McElvogue, D. M. 1999. *La Lavia, La Juliana* and the *Santa María de Vison*: three Spanish Armada transports lost off Streedagh Strand, Co Sligo: an interim report. The International Journal of Nautical Archaeology 28.3: 265-276.

Blanchette, R. A., Nilsson, T., Daniel, G., Abad, A. 1990. Biological degradation of wood. In R. M. Rowell, R. J. Barbour (eds), *Archaeological Wood: Properties, Chemistry, and Preservation*: 141-174. Advances in Chemistry 225. Washington D.C., American Chemical Society.

Björdal, C. G. and Gregory, D., eds. 2011. *WreckProtect: Decay and Protection of Archaeological Wooden Shipwrecks.* Oxford, Archaeopress.

Bojakowski, P. and Custer-Bojakowski, K. 2017. *Warwick*: Report on the excavation of an early 17th-century English shipwreck in Castle Harbour, Bermuda. *International Journal of Nautical Archaeology* 46: 284-302.

Borgin, K., Parameswaran, N. and Liese, W. 1975. The effect of aging on the ultrastructure of wood. *Wood Science and Technology* 9: 87-98.

Bowens, A., ed. 2009. *Underwater Archaeology: The NAS guide to principles and practice.* 2nd edition. West Sussex: Nautical Archaeology Society and Blackwell Publishing.

Brewer, P. & Jansma, E. 2016. *Dendrochronological Data in Archaeology: A Guide to Good Practice. Version 1.1.* Archaeological Data Service / Digital Antiquity: Guides to Good Practice: http://guides.archaeologydataservice.ac.uk/g2gp/Dendro_Toc. Last accessed 20 July 2017.

Bridge, M. 2010. Resource exploitation and wood mobility in Northern European oak: Dendroprovenancing of individual timbers of the *Mary Rose* (1510/11-1545). *International Journal of Nautical Archaeology* 40.2: 417-423.

Bridge, M. 2012. Locating the origins of wood sources: A review of dendroprovenancing. Journal of Archaeological Science 39.8: 2828-2834.

Brodie, N. and Tubb, K. W., eds. 2002. *Illicit Antiquities: The Theft of Culture and the Extinction of Archaeology.* One World Archaeology 42. London, Routledge.

Brodie, N., Kersel, M. M., Luke, C., and Tubb, K. W., eds. 2006. *Archaeology, Cultural Heritage, and the Antiquities Trade.* Gainesville, University Press of Florida.

Brown, D. H. 2011 [2007]. *Archaeological Archives: A Guide to Best Practice in Creation, Compilation, Transfer and Curation.* London: Archaeological Archives Forum, Museum of London.

Butterfields. 2000. *Treasures from the Hoi An Hoard. Important Vietnamese Ceramics from a Late 15th / Early 16th Century Cargo, Volumes 067A and 067B, Sale 7130O.* San Francisco, Butterfields.

Casabán, J. L. 2017. *Santiago de Galicia* and the Illyrian squadron: Characteristics, dimensions and tonnages of Mediterranean-built galleons for Philip's II Atlantic fleets (1593-1597). *The International Journal of Maritime History* 29.2: 238-260.

Casale, G. 2007. The ethnic composition of Ottoman ship crews and the 'Rumi Challenge' to Portuguese identity. *Medieval Encounters* 13: 122-144.

Casale, G. 2010. *The Ottoman Age of Exploration.* Oxford, Oxford.

Castro, F. 2005. *The Pepper Wreck: A Portuguese Indiaman at the Mouth of the Tagus River.* College Station, Texas A & M.

Castro, F. 2008. In search of unique Iberian ship design concepts. *Historical Archaeology* 42: 63-87.

Castro, F. n.d. Treasure hunting: Frequently asked questions. http://nautarch.tamu.edu/shiplab/treasurehunters_04faqs.htm. Last accessed 26 July 2017.

Castro, L., Crespo Solana, A., Farias, I., Martins, A., Monteiro, A., Nayling, N., and Biscaia, F. 2015. *Belinho 1 Shipwreck Timber Catalogue.* Esposende. http://forseadiscovery.eu/sites/default/files/attachments/documents/belinho_1_shipwreck_timber_catalogue_201.pdf. Last accessed 13 August 2017.

Chen, H., Ferrari, C., Angiuli, M., Yao, J., Raspi, C., Bramanti, E. 2010. Qualitative and quantitative analysis of wood samples by Fourier transform infrared spectroscopy and multivariate analysis. *Carbohydrate Polymers* 82: 772–778.

CifA. 2014. *Code of Conduct.* Reading, Chartered Institute for Archaeologists.

Coben, L. A. 2015. The events that led to the Treaty of Tordesillas. *Terrae Incognitae* 47.2: 142-162.

Coles, J. M. and Goodburn, D. M., eds. 1991. *Wet Site Excavation and Survey: Proceedings of a Conference at the Museum of London, October 1990.* Exeter: Wetlands Archaeology Research Papers.

Colombini, M.P., Orlandi, M., Modugno, F., Tolppa, E.-L., Sardelli, M., Zoia, L., and Crestini, C. 2007. Archaeological wood characterisation by PY/GC/MS, GC/MS, NMR and GPC techniques. *Microchemical Journal* 85: 164-173.

Creasman, P. P. 2012. Nautical dendrochronology: an assessment of the whaler *Charles W. Morgan*. In B. Jordan and T. Nowak (eds), *ACUA Underwater Archaeology Proceedings from the Society for Historical Archaeology's Annual Meeting 2012*: 5-12. Columbus, Advisory Council on Underwater Archaeology.

Creasman, P. P., Baisan, C., and Guiterman, C. 2015. Dendrochronological evaluation of ship timber from Charlestown Navy Yard (Boston, MA). *Dendrochronologia* 33: 34-41.

Crespo Solana, A. 2012. Self-organizing: the case of merchant cooperation in the Hispanic Atlantic economy (1680-1778). *Journal of Knowledge Management, Economics and Information Technology*, special issue: Self-Organizing Networks and GIS Tools: Cases of Use for the Study of Trading Cooperation (1400-1800): 191-224.

Crespo Solana, A. 2014. *Spatio-Temporal Narratives: Historical GIS and the Study of Global Trading Networks (1500-1800).* Cambridge, Cambridge.

Crespo Solana, A. 2015. Wood resources, shipbuilding and social environment: The historical context of the ForSEAdiscovery Project. *Skyllis* 15: 52-61.

Crespo Solana, A. and Nayling, N. 2016. ForSEAdiscovery: Forest resources for Iberian empires – Ecology and globalization in the Age of Discovery (16th-18th centuries). *Actas del V Congreso Internacional de Arqueología Subacuática (IKUWA V). Un Patrimonio para la Humanidad, Cartagena*: 896-904. Madrid, Ministerio de Educación, Cultura y Deporte.

Crone, A. and Barber, J. 1981. Analytical techniques for the investigation of non-artefactual wood from prehistoric and medieval sites. *Proceedings of the Society of Antiquaries of Scotland* 111: 510-515.

Croome, A. 1999. Museum Report: The Viking Ship Museum at Roskilde: expansion uncovers nine more early ships; and advances experimental ocean-sailing plans. *International Journal of Nautical Archaeology* 28: 382-393.

Crumlin-Pedersen, O. 1995. Experimental archaeology and ships – bridging the arts and the sciences. *International Journal of Nautical Archaeology* 24: 303-306.

Crumlin-Pedersen, O. and Olsen, O., eds. 2002. *The Skuldelev Ships I: Topography, Archaeology, History, Conservation and Display*. Roskilde: Viking Ship Museum.

Daly, A. 2007. *Timber, Trade and Tree-Rings: A Dendrochronological Analysis of Structural Oak Timber in Northern Europe, c. AD 1000 to c. AD 1650*. Unpublished PhD thesis. University of Southern Denmark.

Daly, A. and Nymoen, P. 2008. The Bøle Ship, Skien, Norway – research, history, dendrochronology and provenance. *International Journal of Nautical Archaeology* 37: 253-170.

de Aranda y Antón, G. 1990. *Los bosques flotantes: historia de un roble del siglo XVIII.* Madrid, Instituto Nacional para la Conservación de la Naturaleza, ICONA.

de Aranda y Antón, G. 1992. Las maderas de América en la arquitectura naval del siglo XVII, Revista de Historia Naval 38: 7-31.

de Aranda y Antón, G. 1999. *La carpintería y la industria naval en el siglo XVIII.* Cuadernos Monográficos del Instituto de Historia y Cultura Naval 33. Madrid, Instituto de Historia Naval.

Deguilloux, M.-F., Pemonge, M.-H., and Petit, R. J. 2004. DNA-based control of oak wood geographic origin in the context of the cooperage industry. *Annals of Forest Science* 61: 97-104.

Demesticha, S. 2011. The 4th-century-BC Mazotos Shipwreck, Cyprus: A preliminary report. *International Journal of Nautical Archaeology* 40: 39-59.

Demesticha, S., Skarlatos, D., and Neophytou, A. 2014. The 4th-century B.C. shipwreck at Mazotos, Cyprus: New techniques and methodologies in the 3D mapping of shipwreck excavations. *Journal of Field Archaeology* 39.2: 134-150.

Domínguez-Delmás, M. 2013. Avances de la dendrocronología al servicio de la arqueología subacuática española: ¿qué información podemos extraer de la madera de los pecios? In X. Nieto Prieto, A. Ramírez Pernia, and P. Recio Sánchez (eds), *Actas del I Congreso de Arqueología Náutica y Subacuática Española. Cartagena, 14, 15 y 16 de marzo de 2013*: 1080-1095. Madrid, Ministerio de Educación, Cultura y Deporte.

Domínguez-Delmás, M., Nayling, N., Waszny, T., Loureiro, V., and Lavier, C. 2013. Dendrochronological dating and provenancing of timbers from the Arade 1 Shipwreck, Portugal. *The International Journal of Nautical Archaeology* 42.1: 118-136.

Domínguez-Delmás, M., Alejano-Monge, R., Van Daalen, S., Rodríguez-Trobajo, E., García González, I., Susperregi, J., Wazny, T., and Jansma, E. 2015. Tree-rings, forest history & cultural heritage: Current state and future prospects of dendroarchaeology in the Iberian Peninsula. *Journal of Archaeological Science* 57: 180-196.

Domínguez-Delmás, M., Groenendijk, P., García-González, I. In preparation, a. Oak and pine tree-ring chronologies to establish the date and provenance of Iberian shipwreck timbers.

Domínguez-Delmás, M., Daly, A., Haneca, K., Nayling, N., and Rich, S. A. In preparation, b. Selecting and sampling shipwreck timbers for dendrochronological research: practical guidance.

Dromgoole, S. 2002. Law and the underwater cultural heritage: A question of balancing interests. In N. Brodie and K. W. Tubb (eds), *Illicit Antiquities: The Theft of Culture and the Extinction of Archaeology*: 109-136. One World Archaeology 42. London, Routledge.

Dromgoole, S. 2013. *Underwater Cultural Heritage and International Law.* Cambridge, Cambridge University Press.

Dumolin-Lapègue, S., Pemonge, M.-H., Gielly, L., Taberlet, P., and Petit, R. J. 1999. Amplification of oak DNA from ancient and modern wood. *Molecular Ecology* 8: 2137-2140.

Durand, S. R., Shelley, P. H., Antweiler, R. C., and Taylor, H. E. 1999. Trees, chemistry, and prehistory in the American Southwest. *Journal of Archaeological Science* 26: 185-203.

Eckstein, D. & S. Wrobel. 2007. Dendrochronological proof of origin of historic timber – retrospect and perspectives. In K. Haneca, A. Verheyden, H. Beekmann, H. Gärtner, G. Helle, and G. Schleser (eds), *TRACE - Tree Rings in Archaeology, Climatology and Ecology, Vol. 5: Proceedings of the DENDROSYMPOSIUM 2006, April 20th – 22nd 2006, Tervuren, Belgium. Schriften des Forschungszentrums Jülich, Reihe Umwelt* 74: 8-20.

English, N. B., Betancourt, J. L., Dean, J. S. & Quade, J. 2001. Strontium isotopes reveal distant sources of architectural timber in Chaco Canyon, New Mexico. *Proceedings of the National Academy of Sciences, U.S.A.* 98: 11891-11896.

Fenwick, V. and A. Gale. 1998. *Historic Shipwrecks: Discovered, Protected & Investigated.* Stroud: Tempus.

Flatman, J. 2009. *Ships and Shipping in Medieval Manuscripts.* London: British Library.

Flecker, M. 2002. The ethics, politics and realities of maritime archaeology in Southeast Asia. *The International Journal of Nautical Archaeology* 31.1: 12–24.

Gallhagher, N. 2016. A methodology for estimating the volume of Baltic timber to Spain using the Sound Toll Registers: 1670-1806. *The International Journal of Maritime History.* 28.4: 752- 773.

Giachi G., Lazzeri, S., Mariotti Lippi, M., Macchioni, N., Paci, S. 2003. The wood of 'C' and 'F' Roman ships found in the ancient harbour of Pisa (Tuscany, Italy): The utilization of different timbers and the probable geographical area which supplied them. *Journal of Cultural Heritage* 4: 269-283.

Giraldez, A. 2015. *The Age of Trade: The Manila Galleons and the Dawn of the Global Economy.* Lanham, Boulder, New York, London, Rowman & Littlefield.

Gómez-Zeledón, J., Grasse, W., Runge, F., Land, A., and Spring, O. 2017. TaqMan qPCR pushes boundaries for the analysis of millennial wood. *Journal of Archaeological Science* 79: 53-61.

Gordon, S. 2015. *A History of the World in Sixteen Shipwrecks.* Lebanon, University Press of New England.

Gosz, J. R. & Moore, D. I. 1989. Strontium isotope studies of atmospheric inputs to forested watersheds in New Mexico. *Biogeochemistry* 8:115-134.

Graustein, W. C. & Armstrong, R. L. 1983. The use of strontium-87/strontium-86 ratios to measure atmospheric transport into forested watersheds. *Science* 219: 289-292.

Guérin, U. and Egger, B. 2010. Guaranteeing the protection of submerged archaeological sites regardless of their location: The UNESCO Convention on the Protection of the Underwater Cultural Heritage (2001). *Journal of Maritime Archaeology* 5: 97-103.

Guibal, F. & Pomey, P. 2003. Timber supply and ancient naval architecture. In C. Beltrame (ed.), *9th International Symposium on Boat and Ship Archaeology: Boats, Ships, and Shipyards. Venice, Italy, 2000*: 35-41. Oxford, Oxbow.

Guibal, F. & Pomey, P. 2004. Dendrochronologie et construction navale antique. *Revue d'Archéométrie* 28: 35-42.

Guilló, M. J. M. 1989. 'A la Mar Madera': La madera en la arquitectura naval española. *Actas IX Jornadas De Andalucta Y América*: 145-171.

Hamdani, A. 1997. An Islamic background to the voyages of discovery. In S. K. Jayyusi (ed.), *The Legacy of Muslim Spain*, vol. 1: 273-304. Leiden, Boston & Koln, Brill.

Hamilton, D. L. 1996. *Basic Methods of Conserving Underwater Archaeological Material Culture.* College Station: Texas A & M. Washington D.C.: U.S. Department of Defense.

Haneca, K. & Daly, A. 2014. Tree-rings, timbers and trees: A dendrochronological survey of the 14th-century cog, Doel 1. *International Journal of Nautical Archaeology* 43: 87-102.

Harpster, M. 2013. Shipwreck identity, methodology, and nautical archaeology. *Journal of Archaeological Method and Theory* 20: 588-622.

Hayes, D. 2001. *Historical Atlas of the North Pacific Ocean. Maps of Discovery and Scientific Exploration 1500-2000.* London, British Museum Press.

Health and Safety Executive. 2014 [1998]. Scientific and archaeological diving projects. Diving at work regulations 1997. Approved code of practice and guidance. http://www.hse.gov.uk/pubns/books/l107.htm. Last accessed on 30/11/2017.

Historic England. 2015a [1998]. Dendrochronology: Guidelines on producing and interpreting dendrochronological dates. Prepared by J. Hillam. https://www.historicengland.org.uk/images-books/publications/dendrochronology-guidelines/. Last accessed on 19/7/2017.

Historic England. 2015b [2006]. Management of Research Projects in the Historic Environment. Prepared by Edmund Lee. http://historicengland.org.uk/images-books/publications/morphe-project-managers-guide/. Last accessed 24/11/2015.

Historic England. 2015c [2010a]. Waterlogged Wood: Guidelines on the recording, sampling, conservation and curation of waterlogged wood. Prepared by Richard Brunning and Jacqui Watson. https://www.historicengland.org.uk/images-books/publications/waterlogged-wood/. Last accessed 11/11/2015.

Historic England. 2015d [2010b]. Accessing England's Protected Wreck Sites: Guidance notes for divers and archaeologists. Prepared by Mark Dunkley and Alison James. https://www.historicengland.org.uk/images-books/publications/accessing-englands-protected-wreck-sites-guidance-notes/. Last accessed 11/11/2015.

Historic England. 2015e [2014]. Marine Licensing and England's Historic Environment. Marine Planning Unit. https://historicengland.org.uk/images-books/publications/marine-licensing-and-englands-historic-environment/. Last accessed 18 July 2017.

Hughes, M. K., Milsom, S. J., and Leggett, P. A. 1981. Sapwood estimates in the interpretation or tree-ring dates. *Journal of Archaeological Science* 8: 381-390.

Huysecom, E., Hajdas, I., Renold, M.-A., Synal, H.-A., and Mayor, A. 2017. The 'enhancement' of cultural heritage by AMS dating: ethical questions. *Radiocarbon* 59.2: 559-563.

Isorena, E. B. 2015. Maritime disasters in Spanish Philippines: The Manila-Acapulco galleons, 1565-1815. *International Journal of Asia-Pacific Studies* 11.1: 53-83.

Jiao, L., Liu, X., Jiang, X. & Yin, Y. 2015. Extraction and amplification of DNA from aged and archaeological *Populus euphratica* wood for species identification. *Holzforschung* 69.8: 925-932.

Jiao, L., Yin, Y., Cheng, Y. & Jiang, X. 2014. DNA barcoding for identification of the endangered species *Aquilaria sinensis*: Comparison of data from heated or aged wood samples.' *Holzforschung* 68: 487-494.

JNAPC. 2007. *Underwater Finds. Guidance for Divers*. http://www.jnapc.org.uk/Underwater%20Finds%20Booklet.pdf. Last accessed 20 July 2017. York, Joint Nautical Archaeology Policy Committee.

Jones, A. 2004. Archaeology and materiality: Materials-based analysis in theory and practice. *Archaeometry* 46: 327-338.

Jones, T. 2009. *The Newport Medieval Ship: Timber Recording Manual*. Archaeology Data Service. http://archaeologydataservice.ac.uk/. Last accessed 25/11/2015.

Juvelier, B. 2017. 'Salvaging' history: Underwater cultural heritage and commercial salvage. *American University International Law Review* 32.5: 1024-1045.

Keith, D. H. and Simmons III, J. J. 1985. Analysis of hull remains, ballast, and artifact distribution of a 16th-century shipwreck, Molasses Reef, British West Indies. *Journal of Field Archaeology* 12: 4111-424.

Kelsey, H. 2016. *The First Circumnavigators: Unsung Heroes of the Age of Discovery*. New Haven & London, Harvard University Press.

Khanjian, H., Schilling, M. & Maish, J. 2013. FTIR and Py-GC/MS investigations of archaeological amber objects from the J. Paul Getty Museum. *e-Preservation Science* 10: 66-70.

Krąpiec, M. and Krąpiec, P. 2014. In W. Ossowski (ed), *The Copper Ship: A Medieval Shipwreck and Its Cargo*, 143-160. Gdansk: National Maritime Museum.

Liphschitz, N. 2007. *Timber in Ancient Israel: Dendroarchaeology and Dendrochronology*. Tel Aviv: Tel Aviv University.

Liphschitz, N. 2009. Kyrenia and Ma'agan Mikhael shipwrecks: A comparative dendroarchaeological study. *Skyllis* 9: 18-21.

Liphschitz, N. 2012a. Dendroarchaeological studies of shipwrecks along the Mediterranean coast of Israel. In R. Efe, M. Ozturk and S. Ghazanfar (eds), *Environment and Ecology in the Mediterranean Region*: 1-12. Newcastle-upon-Tyne, Cambridge Scholars.

Liphschitz, N. 2012b. Dendroarchaeology of shipwrecks in Israel. *Bocconea* 24: 95-104.
Loewen, B. & Delhaye, M. 2006. Oak growing, hull design and framing style. The Cavalaire-sur-Mer wreck, c. 1479. In L. Blue, F. Hocker & A. Englert (eds), *Connected by Sea: Proceedings of the Tenth International Symposium on Boat and Ship Archaeology, Roskilde 2003*: 88-104. Oxford, Oxbow Books.
Loewen, B. 2001. The structures of Atlantic shipbuilding in the 16th century. An archaeological perspective. In F. Alves (ed.), *Proceedings of the International Symposium on Archaeology of Medieval and Modern Ships of Iberian-Atlantic Tradition, Centro Nacional de Arqueologia Náutica e Subaquática, Academia de Marinha Lisboa, September 7. to 9., 1998*: 241-258. Lisbon, Instituto Português Archaeologia.
Loewen, B. 2000. Forestry practices and hull design, ca. 1400-1700. In I. Guerreiro (ed.), *Fernando Oliveira and His Time: Humanism and the Art of Navigation in Renaissance Europe (1450-1650)*, 143-151. Aveiro: Patrimonia Aveiro.
Loewen, B. 1998. Recent advances in ship history and archaeology, 1450-1650: Hull design, regional typologies and wood studies. *Material Culture Review* 48: 1-10.
Lorentzen, B., Manning, S. W., Cvikel, D., and Kahanov, Y. 2014. High-precision dating the Akko 1 shipwreck, Israel: Wiggle-matching the life and death of a ship into the historical record. *Journal of Archaeological Science* 41: 772-783.
Loureiro, V. 2012. Regional characteristics of the Iberian-Atlantic shipbuilding tradition: Arade I shipwreck case study. In N. Günsenin (ed.), *Between Continents: Proceedings of the Twelfth Symposium on Boat and Ship Archaeology, Istanbul 2009*: 233-240. Istanbul, Ege Yayınları.
Lu, B. and Zhou, S. 2016. China's state-led working model on protection of underwater cultural heritage: practice, challenges, and possible solutions. *Marine Policy* 65: 39-47.
Lucas, G. 2001. Destruction and the rhetoric of excavation. *Norwegian Archaeological Review* 34: 35-46.
Lucas, G. 2012. *Understanding the Archaeological Record*. Cambridge: Cambridge University Press.
Łuceijko, J.J., Modugno, F., Ribechini, E. & Del Río, J. C. 2009. Characterisation of archaeological waterlogged wood by pyrolytic and mass spectrometric techniques. *Analytica Chimica Acta* 654.1: 26-34.
Manning, S. W., Dee, M. W., Wild, E. M., Ramsey, C. B., Bandy, K., Creasman, P. P., Griggs, C. B., Pearson, C. L., Shortland, A. J. and Steier, P. 2014. High-precision dendro-^{14}C dating of two cedar wood sequences from First Intermediate Period and Middle Kingdom Egypt and a small regional climate-related ^{14}C divergence. *Journal of Archaeological Science* 46: 401-416.
Martin, C. 1990. The ships of the Spanish Armada. In P. Gallagher and D. W. Cruickshank (eds), *Gods Obvious Design: Papers for the Spanish Armada Symposium, Sligo, 1988, with an Edition and Translation of the Account of Francisco de Cuéllar*, 41-68. London: Tamesis Books Limited.
Martin, C. 2001. De-particularizing the particular: approaches to the investigation of well-documented post-medieval shipwrecks. *World Archaeology* 33.3: 383-399.
Martins, A., Almeida, A., Magalhães, I., Castro, F., Bezant, J., Domínguez-Delmás, M., Nayling, N., and Groenendijk, P. In press. Reconstructing trees from ship timber assemblages using 3D modelling technologies: Evidence from the Belinho 1 shipwreck in Northern Portugal. *IKUWA VI Conference Proceedings*. Fremantle Australia.
Matar, N. 1999. *Turks, Moors, and Englishmen in the Age of Discovery*. New York, Columbia University Press.
Mathewson III, R. D. 1986. *Treasure of the Atocha*. New York, Pisces Books.
Meiggs, R. 1982. *Trees and Timber in the Ancient Mediterranean World*. Oxford, Oxford.
Monchet, K. T. and Santos, A. 2015. Forestry and timber supply in the royal forests of the Iberian Peninsula through the 16th century. *Skyllis* 15: 62-68.
Muller, S. D. 2005. Palynological study of Antique shipwrecks from the western Mediterranean Sea, France. *Journal of Archaeological Science* 31.3: 343-349.
Nautical Archaeology Society. n.d. Understanding the Law. http://www.nauticalarchaeologysociety.org/content/understanding-law. Last accessed 27 July 2017.
Nayling, N. & Susperregi, J. 2014. Iberian dendrochronology and the Newport Medieval Ship. *International Journal of Nautical Archaeology* 43: 279-291.

Niven, K. and Pierce-McManamon, F., eds. 2011. *Guides to Good Practice.* Archaeology Data Service / Digital Antiquity. http://guides.archaeologydataservice.ac.uk/g2gp/Main. Last accessed 14/11/2015.

Noonan, F. T. 2007. *The Road to Jerusalem: Pilgrimage and Travel in the Age of Discovery.* Philadelphia, University of Pennsylvania Press.

Oertling, T. J. 1989. The Highborn Cay wreck: The 1986 field season. *International Journal of Nautical Archaeology* 18.3: 244-253.

Oertling, T. 2001. The concept of the Atlantic vessel. In F. Alves (ed.), *Proceedings of the International Symposium on Archaeology of Medieval and Modern Ships of Iberian-Atlantic Tradition, Centro Nacional de Arqueologia Náutica e Subaquática, Academia de Marinha Lisboa, September 7. to 9., 1998*: 233-240. Lisbon, Instituto Português Archaeologia.

O'Keefe, P. J. 2013. 'Commerical exploitation': its prohibition in the UNESCO Convention on Protection of the Underwater Cultural Heritage 2001 and other instruments. *Art, Antiquity & Law* 18.2: 129-148.

Orton, C. 2000. *Sampling in Archaeology.* Cambridge, Cambridge.

Palma, P. and L. N. Santhakumaran. 2014. *Shipwrecks and Global 'Worming'.* Oxford, Archaeopress.

Perlin, J. A. 1989. *A Forest Journey: The Role of Wood in the Development of Civilization.* New York, W. W. Norton.

Phillips, C. R. 1986. *Six Galleons for the King of Spain.* Baltimore, The Johns Hopkins University Press.

Piquette, K. E. and Crowther, C. 2011. Developing a reflectance transformation imaging (RTI) system for inscription documentation in museum collections and the field. Case studies on ancient Egyptian and Classical material. http://www.digitalclassicist.org/wip/wip2011-01kp.pdf. Last accessed 19 July 2017.

Plets, R. M. K., Dix, J. K. and Best, A. I. 2007. Mapping of the buried Yarmouth Roads wreck, Isle of Wight, UK, using a chirp sub-bottom profiler. *International Journal of Nautical Archaeology* 37: 360-373.

Pollard, A. M. 2011. Isotopes and impact: a cautionary tale. *Antiquity* 85: 631-638.

Polónia, A. and Barros, A. 2012. Commercial flows and transference patterns between Iberian empires (16th-17th centuries). *Journal of Knowledge Management, Economics and Information Technology*, special issue: Self-Organizing Networks and GIS Tools: Cases of Use for the Study of Trading Cooperation (1400-1800): 111-144.

Pope, F. 2007. *Dragon Sea: A True Tale of Treasure, Archaeology and Greed off the Coast of Vietnam.* London, Harcourt Inc.

Rich, S. A. 2017. *Cedar Forests, Cedar Ships: Allure, Lore, and Metaphor in the Mediterranean Near East.* Oxford, Archaeopress.

Rich, S. A., Manning, S. W., Degryse, P., Vanhaecke, F. & Van Lerberghe, K. 2012. Tree-ring and strontium isotope signatures of *Cedrus brevifolia* in Cyprus. *Journal of Analytical Atomic Spectrometry* 27: 796-806.

Rich, S., Satchell, J., and Mason, B. 2015. *Yarmouth Roads Protected Wreck. Licensee Report 2015.* Unpublished report prepared by the Maritime Archaeology Trust for Historic England.

Rich, S. A., Manning, S. W., Degryse, P., Vanhaecke, F. & Van Lerberghe, K. 2015. Provenancing East Mediterranean cedar wood with the $^{87}Sr/^{86}Sr$ strontium isotope ratio. *Journal of Archaeological and Anthropological Sciences* 8: 467-476.

Rich, S. A., Manning, S. W., Degryse, P., Vanhaecke, F., Latruwe, K., & Van Lerberghe, K. 2016. Putting a cedar ship in a bottle: Dendroprovenance results of three ancient East Mediterranean vessels. *Journal of Archaeological Science Reports* 9: 514-521.

Rich, S. and Satchell, J. 2016. *Yarmouth Roads Protected Wreck. Licensee Report 2016.* Unpublished Report prepared by the Maritime Archaeology Trust for Historic England.

Rich, S., Momber, G., and Nayling, N. In press. Maritime archaeological timber sampling: Methods and results from the silty Solent. *IKUWA6 Proceedings.* Freemantle, Australia.

Richards, J. 2006. *The Unending Frontier: An Environmental History of the Early Modern World.* Oakland, University of California Press.

Rival, M. 1991. *La Charpenterie Navale Romaine: Matériaux, Méthodes, Moyens.* Paris, Editions du Centre National de la Recherche Scientifique.

Ruano, A. A. 2013. Guided pollards and the Basque woodland during the Early Modern Age. In I. Rotherham (ed.), *Cultural Severance and the Environment*. Environmental History, volume 2. Dordrecht, Springer.

Sadori, L., Bertini, A., Combourieu-Nebout, N., Kouli, K., Mariotti Lippi, M., Roberts, N. Mercuri A. M. 2013. Palynology and Mediterranean vegetation history. *Flora Mediterranea* 23: 141-156.

Schoch, W., Heller, I., Schweingruber, F.H., Kienast,F., 2004, *Wood Anatomy of Central European Species*. www.woodanatomy.ch. Last accessed 3 August 2017.

Schweingruber, F. H. 2012. *Trees and Wood in Dendrochronology: Morphological, Anatomical, and Tree-Ring Analytical Characteristics of Trees Frequently Used in Dendrochronology*. Berlin, Springer-Verlag.

Smith, R. C., Keith, D. H., and Lakey, D. 1985. The Highborn Cay wreck: Further exploration of a 16th-century Bahaman shipwreck. *International Journal of Nautical Archaeology* 14.1: 63-72.

Sohar, K., Vitas, A., and Läänelaid, A. 2012. Sapwood estimates of pedunculated oak (*Quercus robur* L.) in the eastern Baltic. *Dendrochronologia* 30: 49-56.

Speirs, A. K., McConnachie, G. & Lowe, A. J. 2009. Chloroplast DNA from 16th century waterlogged oak in a marine environment: initial steps in sourcing the Mary Rose timbers. In M. Haslam, G. Robertson, A. Crowther, S. Nugent & L. Kirkwood (eds), *Archaeological Science Under a Microscope: Studies in Residue and Ancient DNA Analysis in Honour of Thomas H. Loy* (Terra Australis 30): 175-189. Canberra, ANU Press.

Steffy, J. R. 2001. The development of ancient and medieval shipbuilding techniques. In F. Alves (ed.), *Proceedings of the International Symposium on Archaeology of Medieval and Modern Ships of Iberian-Atlantic Tradition, Centro Nacional de Arqueologia Náutica e Subaquática, Academia de Marinha Lisboa, September 7. to 9., 1998*: 49-61. Lisbon, Instituto Português Archaeologia.

Stelzner, J. and Million, S. 2015. X-ray Computed Tomography for the anatomical and dendrochronological analysis of archaeological wood. *Journal of Archaeological Science* 55: 188-196.

Throckmorton, P. 1998. The world's worst investment. In L. E. Babits and H. Van Tilburg (eds), *Maritime Archaeology*: 75-83. The Springer Series in Underwater Archaeology. Boston, Springer.

Traoré, M., Kaal, J. & Cortizas A. M. 2016. Application of FTIR spectroscopy to the characterization of archaeological wood. *Spectrochimica Acta Part A: Molecular and Biomolecular Spectroscopy* 153: 63-70.

Trindade, A. R., Domínguez-Delmás, M., Traoré, M., Gallagher, N., Rich, S. A., Martins, A. M. In press. From forests to the sea, from the sea to the laboratory: the timbers of the frigate *Santa María Magdalena* (18th century). *IKUWA6 Proceedings*. Freemantle, Australia.

Maarleveld, T., Guerin, U., and Egger, B (eds). 2013. Manual for Activities Directed at Underwater Cultural Heritage: Guidelines to the Annex of the UNESCO 2001 Convention. Paris, UNESCO.

Vermeersch, J. and Haneca, K. 2015. Construction features of Doel 1, a 14th-century cog found in Flanders. *International Journal of Nautical Archaeology* 44.1: 111-131.

Vermeersch, J., Haneca, K., and Daly, A. 2015. Doel 2: a second 14th-century cog wrecked in den Deurganck, Doel, Belgium. *International Journal of Nautical Archaeology* 44.2: 327-348.

Vivas Pinedas, G. 1998. Legiones de madera: la contrucción naval al servicio de la Compañía Guipuzcoana de Caracas. *Itsas Memoria. Revista de Estudios Marítimios del País Vasco*, 2: 267-295. Donostia - San Sebastian, Untzi Museoa - Museo Naval.

Waisberg, T. 2017. The Treaty of Tordesillias and the (re)invention of international law in the Age of Discovery. *Meridiano* 47, 18: e18003.

Watson, K. and Gale, A. 1990. Site evaluation for marine site and monuments records: The Yarmouth Roads wreck investigation. *International Journal of Nautical Archaeology* 19: 183-192.

Wazny, T. 2005. The origin, assortments and transport of Baltic timber: historic-dendrochronological evidence. In C. Van de Velde, H. Beeckman, J. Van Ackerand, and F. Verhaeghe (eds), *Constructing Wooden Images: Proceedings of the Symposium oon the Organization of Labour and Working Practices of Late Gothic Carved Altarpieces in the Low Countries, Brussels, 25-26 October 2002*: 115-126. Brussels, Vrije Universiteit.

Wazny, T. 2011. Dendro-provenancing between the Baltic Sea and the East Mediterranean. In P. Fraiture (ed.), *Tree Rings, Art, Archaeology: Proceedings of a Conference*: 81-87. Turnhout, Brepols.

Wicha, S. 2005. *Caractérisation d'un groupe d'épaves antiques de Méditerranée présentant un assemblage des membrures par ligatures végétales: Approche architecturale et paléobotanique.* Ph.D. thesis. Universities of Aix-Marseille and Provence.

Wilson, M. A., Godfrey, I. M, Hanna, J. V., Quezada, R. A., Finnie, K. S. 1993. The degradation of wood in old Indian-Ocean shipwrecks. *Organic Geochemistry* 20: 599–610.

Wing, J. T. 2015. *Roots of Empire: Forests and State Power in Early Modern Spain, c. 1500-1750.* Leiden: Brill.

Yarrow, T. 2010. In context: meaning, materiality and agency in the process of archaeological recording. In C. Knappet & M. Lambros (eds), *Material Agency: Towards a Non-Anthropocentric Approach*: 121-137. New York, Springer.